PIZZA
&
PASTA

Pizza & Pasta

TRADITIONAL AND
CONTEMPORARY RECIPES
FOR PERFECT PIZZAS,
PASTA & MORE

This edition published in 2011

LOVE FOOD is an imprint of Parragon Books Ltd

Parragon
Queen Street House
4 Queen Street
Bath BA1 1HE, UK

ISBN: 978-1-4454-4449-9

Printed in China

Authors: Ingebrog Pils, Stefan Pallmer
Introduction: Linda Doeser
Photography: Martin Kurtenbach, Buenavista Studio

Notes for the Reader
This book uses both metric and imperial measurements. Follow the
same units of measurement throughout; do not mix metric and
imperial. All spoon measurements are level: teaspoons are assumed
to be 5 ml, and tablespoons are assumed to be 15 ml. Unless otherwise
stated, milk is assumed to be full fat, eggs and individual vegetables
are medium, and pepper is freshly ground black pepper.

The times given are an approximate guide only. Preparation times
differ according to the techniques used by different people and the
cooking times may also vary from those given. Optional ingredients,
variations or serving suggestions have not been included in the
calculations.

Recipes using raw or very lightly cooked eggs should be avoided by
infants, the elderly, pregnant women, convalescents and anyone
suffering from an illness. Pregnant and breastfeeding women are
advised to avoid eating peanuts and peanut products. Sufferers
from nut allergies should be aware that some of the ready-made
ingredients used in the recipes in this book may contain nuts. Always
check the packaging before use.

CONTENTS

INTRODUCTION

Italian food, whether it's a fabulous seafood salad, a rich veal stew, a vegetable frittata or a frothy dessert, is renowned throughout the world for its superb flavour, emphasis on freshness and subtle simplicity. However, the crown for the best known and most widely loved of all Italian culinary creations must be shared by pizza and pasta.

The story of Italian cooking is the story of the country itself – its political and economic history, geographical and climatic variety, rural traditions, cultural heritage, and a kind of powerful local patriotism known as *campanismo*. Foreign invasion, exploration and trade influenced the indigenous cuisine and introduced new ingredients, most notably, those Italian staples – tomatoes, peppers and chillies – from the New World.

Pizza

Pizza is the perfect illustration of this – a simple, filling and economical dish, made with a few basic ingredients, created by the poor, but ingenious and spirited, people of Naples in rural Campania. Nowadays it usually features tomatoes and traditional toppings include local, seasonal ingredients such as onions, artichokes, olives and, of course, mozzarella cheese. It is always delicately seasoned with herbs – in fact, the word pizza comes from the verb *pizzicare*, to sting or season. Local peasants had been preparing pizzas flavoured simply with herbs, garlic and olive oil for decades before the introduction of tomatoes in the eighteenth century and the first written recipe did not appear for another 150 years. Even then, it would have remained an Italian secret if poverty had not forced huge waves of emigration in the nineteenth and early twentieth centuries. Neapolitans took their culinary traditions to their new homes, especially New York, and in doing so introduced pizza to the world.

Even Italians from other regions acknowledge that pizza is a Neapolitan speciality and are proud of it and its global popularity, although they are bemused by some of its guises in other countries. Some years ago the Italian ambassador in London made an impassioned plea for foreigners to stop using non-traditional toppings on pizzas to protect the integrity and authenticity of this classic dish.

Pasta

While the origins of pizza are well known, pasta's pedigree is less clear. The legend that it was brought from China by the Venetian traveller Marco Polo in the thirteenth century is appealing, but almost certainly not true. There is evidence that pasta was made in pre-Roman Italy and similar doughs were also being made in other parts of Europe. The first written evidence for Italian pasta – actually from Sicily – dates from the Middle Ages but there is no doubt that it had been a staple food for a long time before that.

Like pizza, pasta is a typical example of the story of Italian cooking. It is filling, nourishing and inexpensive and, in the hands of Italy's inventive cooks, could be partnered with an almost infinite number of sauces made from all kinds of seasonal and local produce. It is a product of southern Italy where durum wheat is an important crop. This is ground into the fine semolina flour that is used to make pasta. By contrast, the northern staple crop is rice. The Saracen invasion of Sicily in the ninth century also contributed to the development of this now world-famous food. A sophisticated system of irrigation vastly improved the production of durum wheat and the Saracens also introduced new ingredients such as spinach and almonds. It seems, too, that they invented spaghetti, or at least tubular pasta, and developed a technique for drying it. However, it was the Neapolitans who perfected the technique, exploiting the warm, dry climate of Campania which was also ideal for growing durum wheat. Nowadays, of course, climate has no role in the commercial production of pasta which is dried under controlled conditions in factories that can be sited anywhere in the country.

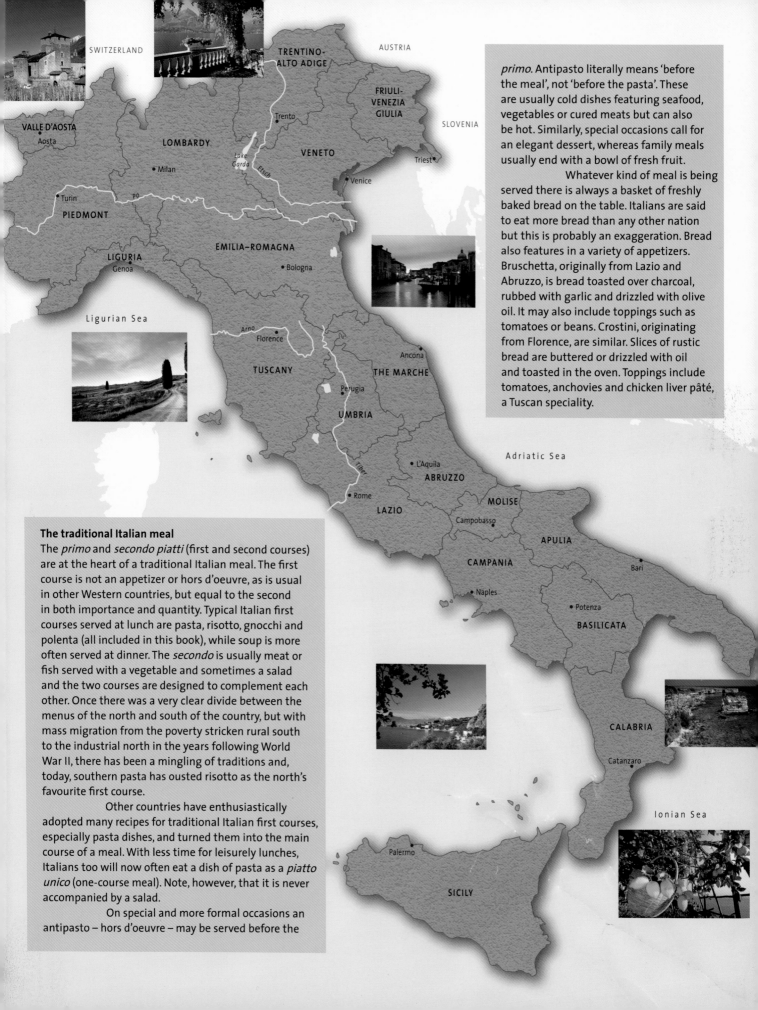

primo. Antipasto literally means 'before the meal', not 'before the pasta'. These are usually cold dishes featuring seafood, vegetables or cured meats but can also be hot. Similarly, special occasions call for an elegant dessert, whereas family meals usually end with a bowl of fresh fruit.

Whatever kind of meal is being served there is always a basket of freshly baked bread on the table. Italians are said to eat more bread than any other nation but this is probably an exaggeration. Bread also features in a variety of appetizers. Bruschetta, originally from Lazio and Abruzzo, is bread toasted over charcoal, rubbed with garlic and drizzled with olive oil. It may also include toppings such as tomatoes or beans. Crostini, originating from Florence, are similar. Slices of rustic bread are buttered or drizzled with oil and toasted in the oven. Toppings include tomatoes, anchovies and chicken liver pâté, a Tuscan speciality.

The traditional Italian meal

The *primo* and *secondo piatti* (first and second courses) are at the heart of a traditional Italian meal. The first course is not an appetizer or hors d'oeuvre, as is usual in other Western countries, but equal to the second in both importance and quantity. Typical Italian first courses served at lunch are pasta, risotto, gnocchi and polenta (all included in this book), while soup is more often served at dinner. The *secondo* is usually meat or fish served with a vegetable and sometimes a salad and the two courses are designed to complement each other. Once there was a very clear divide between the menus of the north and south of the country, but with mass migration from the poverty stricken rural south to the industrial north in the years following World War II, there has been a mingling of traditions and, today, southern pasta has ousted risotto as the north's favourite first course.

Other countries have enthusiastically adopted many recipes for traditional Italian first courses, especially pasta dishes, and turned them into the main course of a meal. With less time for leisurely lunches, Italians too will now often eat a dish of pasta as a *piatto unico* (one-course meal). Note, however, that it is never accompanied by a salad.

On special and more formal occasions an antipasto – hors d'oeuvre – may be served before the

Pizza & Bread

Pizza

There is probably no other dish that is as internationally synonymous with Italian cuisine as the *pizza*, although Italians principally understand it to mean Neapolitan pizza. This is all the more remarkable since pizza is the offspring of peasants' kitchens. Born of necessity, it was the means to concoct a flavourful, satisfying meal from a few very simple ingredients.

The first written pizza recipe dates back to 1858, but Neapolitans were already familiar with it at the beginning of the eighteenth century. Pizza dough with tomatoes was first documented in Naples at the end of the seventeenth century. Pizza's triumphal journey around the globe did not start in Naples, but rather in far away New York City. In 1905, Signore Lombardi opened the first pizzeria in New York's Little Italy neighbourhood. American pizzas, unlike those from pizza's hometown of Naples, were lavishly decked out with a variety of ingredients and soon became a smash hit. Indeed, pizza is one of the Americans' favourite foods: 40 hectares of pizza is consumed every day in the United States!

The thin, flat dough is first covered with flavourful tomato sauce.

Then the pizza is topped with buffalo mozzarella cut into small pieces.

Marinara and Margherita

When King Umberto I of Italy and his wife, Margaret of Savoy, visited the city of Naples on 11 June 1889, she expressed the desire to try a local speciality. In the royal kitchen, pizza baker Raffaele Esposito created a new variation on the ordinary *pizza marinara* for them. *Pizza marinara*, made with garlic, oregano and oil, was chiefly popular among fishermen coming ashore in the early morning after a night at sea. Raffaele regarded this simple garlic pizza as inappropriate and chose ingredients representing the Italian national colours instead: green (basil), white (mozzarella) and red (tomatoes). It was named *pizza margherita* in honour of the queen. She must have been very pleased, because from then on Raffaele was known by the title *Fornitore della Real Casa*, Purveyor to the Royal Court. One of the oldest pizzerias in Naples, the Pizzeria Da Michele, to this day serves nothing but *pizza marinara* and *pizza margherita*.

The One and Only Authentic Neapolitan Pizza

The *Associazione Vera Pizza Napoletana* endeavours to defend Neapolitan pizza against cheap imitations. This organization has established standards for a genuine pizza. An authentic pizza must be made of dough that is kneaded by hand, its crust must be formed and flattened solely by hand, and it must be round. Pizza dough may consist only of flour, yeast, salt and water.

A genuine Neapolitan pizza has a maximum diameter of 30 cm (12 inches), and it must be baked directly on the stone floor of the pizza oven. All deviations from this original recipe 'must lie within the limits of good taste and culinary responsibility'.

Fresh basil leaves and rich, fruity olive oil lend pizzas colour and flavour.

The Pizza Oven

When asked why their pizzas taste so much better than pizzas anywhere else, Italians do not have to think for long before responding. It is still the wood-fired ovens that lend the dough its very special flavour. A genuine pizza oven is dome shaped, and its interior walls are lined with ovenproof (heat-resistant) tiles. In the small village of Maiano near Naples, these ovens have been handmade out of clay from the Sorrento Peninsula since the fifteenth century, using a special technique.

On the stone floor of the pizza oven, a wood fire burns directly on the baking surface. But the fire hardly produces any smoke, because cherry or olive wood are burnt. The flames heat up the tile walls, while the distinctive shape of the oven provides for even distribution of the heat. When fully heated, the burning wood is pushed to the rear of the oven to make room for the pizzas. The glowing embers keep the temperature of the oven at a minimum of 400°C (750°F). At this incredible temperature, the pizza bakes very quickly. In less than a minute, the base of the dough is crisp, the tomatoes are not yet dry, the mozzarella is perfectly melted and the healthy fatty acids in the olive oil have not yet been destroyed.

Piadina

Piadina is to Emilia-Romagna and the northern Marche provinces what pizza is to Naples: a simple and inexpensive dish, eaten in the fingers and enthusiastically accompanied by a small glass of table wine. Piadina consists of wheat flour, lard, salt, bicarbonate of soda and water. Using a rolling pin, the dough is rolled out into thin circles about 20 cm (8 inches) in diameter and then baked, traditionally in a terracotta pan. The finished *piadina* are folded over and cut into four pieces, or rolled up. They are eaten hot with cheese, ham, sausage or salad, and can also be stuffed with sautéed vegetables.

Basic Pizza Dough

40 g/1½ oz compressed fresh yeast or
2 sachets easy-blend dried yeast

½ tsp sugar

400 g/14 oz flour,
plus extra for dusting

1 tsp salt

3 tbsp olive oil

Crumble the yeast into a small bowl and sprinkle with the sugar. Add 125 ml/4 fl oz lukewarm water, then stir to dissolve the yeast and sugar. Cover with a clean tea towel and prove in a warm spot for 30 minutes. Sift the flour into a large bowl. Make a hollow in the centre and pour the yeast mixture, salt, olive oil and 5–7 tablespoons of water into it. Knead everything into a smooth, silky dough, then shape it into a ball. Dust the ball with a little flour, cover and set aside in a warm place to rise for an additional hour, or until doubled in volume.

Pizzette

Pizzette
Small Pizzas

40 g/1½ oz compressed fresh yeast or
2 sachets easy-blend dried yeast

½ tsp sugar

400 g/14 oz flour, plus extra for dusting

1 tsp salt

60 ml/2 fl oz olive oil,
plus extra for greasing

500 g/1 lb 2 oz tomatoes

1 radicchio

100 g/3½ oz bacon, cut into strips

50 g/1¾ oz pine kernels

Crumble the yeast into a small bowl and sprinkle with the sugar. Add 125 ml/4 fl oz lukewarm water, then stir to dissolve the yeast and sugar. Cover with a clean tea towel and prove in a warm spot for 30 minutes. Sift the flour into a large bowl. Make a hollow in the centre and pour the yeast mixture, salt, 3 tablespoons of olive oil and 5–7 tablespoons of water into it. Knead everything into a smooth, silky dough, then shape it into a ball. Dust the ball with a little flour, cover and set aside in a warm place to rise for about 1 hour or until doubled in volume.

Grease two baking sheets with olive oil and preheat the oven to 200°C/390°F/gas mark 6. Peel and quarter the tomatoes, remove the seeds, and cut into small dice. Trim the radicchio and break it into bite-sized pieces.

Divide the dough into 12 equal pieces. Form each into a ball, flatten and place the rounds on the baking sheets. Top with the diced tomato and bacon and drizzle on the remaining oil. Bake for 15 minutes, then sprinkle the radicchio and pine kernels over the *pizzette* and bake for another 5 minutes.

Pizza di patate
Apulian Potato Pizza

750 g/1 lb 10 oz potatoes

1 tsp salt

3 tbsp flour

70 ml/2½ fl oz olive oil,
plus extra for greasing

400 g/14 oz canned peeled tomatoes

100 g/3½ oz black olives

12 anchovies in oil

150 g/5 oz feta cheese, diced

1 onion, cut into rings

2 garlic cloves, finely chopped

½ tsp rosemary

½ tsp dried oregano

freshly ground pepper

Bring a saucepan of salted water to the boil and cook the potatoes. Drain, rinse them in cold water, peel, and put through a potato press while still hot. Stir in the salt, flour and 2 tablespoons of the olive oil and leave the mixture to cool.

Grease a springform cake tin (28 cm/11 inches in diameter) with olive oil and preheat the oven to 220°C/430°F/gas mark 7. Drain the tomatoes and cut them into small pieces. Press the potato dough into the pan, creating a rim. Spread the tomatoes, olives, anchovies, feta cheese, onion and garlic on the dough. Sprinkle with rosemary, oregano and pepper, then bake for approximately 30 minutes.

The Most Popular Pizzas

Pizza con gamberi
Prawn Pizza

1 pizza dough
(see recipe on page 13)
750 g/1 lb 10 oz tomatoes
600 g/1 lb 5 oz cooked prawns, shelled
100 g/3½ oz black olives
2 tsp fennel seeds
4 tbsp olive oil, plus extra for greasing
1 handful rocket
flour for dusting
salt and pepper

Preheat the oven to 225°C/435°F/gas mark 7 and grease four round pizza pans. Peel and quarter the tomatoes, remove the seeds, and cut into small dice. Rinse the prawns and drain well.

Divide the dough into four equal portions and roll them into circles on a floured surface. Place the dough on the pizza pans and top with the tomatoes, prawns and olives. Season with the fennel seeds, salt and pepper and drizzle with the olive oil. Bake for about 20 minutes.

Wash the rocket and remove any coarse stalks. Shortly before serving, distribute the rocket leaves on top of the pizzas.

Pizza Margherita

1 pizza dough
(see recipe on page 13)
75 ml/2½ fl oz olive oil,
plus extra for greasing
2 small onions, diced
400 g/14 oz canned diced tomatoes
50 g/1¾ oz canned tomato sauce
1 tsp oregano
400 g/14 oz mozzarella
salt and pepper
flour for dusting
basil leaves to garnish

Heat 4 tablespoons of the olive oil and sauté the onions until translucent. Add both kinds of tomatoes and the oregano, and season with salt and pepper. Cook the sauce for about 30 minutes on medium heat.

Preheat the oven to 225°C/435°F/gas mark 7 and grease four round pizza pans with olive oil. Divide the dough into four equal portions and roll them into circles on a floured surface. Place the circles of dough on the pizza pans.

Thinly slice the mozzarella. Brush the dough with the tomato sauce, cover with mozzarella slices, and drizzle on the remaining olive oil. Bake for about 20 minutes, then garnish with basil leaves and serve immediately.

Pizza alla marinara
Mariner's Pizza

1 pizza dough
(see recipe on page 13)
800 g/1 lb 12 oz canned diced tomatoes
3–4 garlic cloves, finely chopped
1 tbsp oregano
50 g/1¾ oz capers
100 g/3½ oz black olives
200 g/7 oz Bel Paese cheese, grated
3 tbsp olive oil, plus extra for greasing
flour for dusting
salt
freshly ground pepper

Preheat the oven to 225°C/435°F/gas mark 7 and grease four round pizza pans with olive oil. Divide the dough into four equal portions and roll them into circles on a floured surface. Place the circles of dough on the pizza pans.

Distribute the tomatoes on the dough. Season with the garlic, oregano, salt and pepper. Scatter on the capers and olives and sprinkle with the grated cheese. Drizzle on the olive oil, then bake the pizzas for about 20 minutes.

Pizza quattro stagioni
Four Seasons Pizza

1 pizza dough
(see recipe on page 13)
1 tbsp butter
200 g/7 oz mushrooms, sliced
4 tomatoes
200 g/7 oz cooked ham
200 g/7 oz mozzarella
4 artichoke hearts in oil
16 black olives
1 tsp oregano
4 tbsp olive oil, plus extra for greasing
flour for dusting
salt and pepper

Preheat the oven to 225°C/435°F/gas mark 7 and grease four round pizza pans with olive oil. Heat the butter and sauté the mushrooms for 10 minutes. Peel and quarter the tomatoes, remove the seeds, and cut into small dice. Cut the ham into small pieces. Thinly slice the mozzarella. Quarter the artichoke hearts.

Divide the dough into four equal portions and roll them into circles on a floured surface. Place the circles of dough on the pizza pans.

Distribute the tomatoes and mozzarella evenly on the pizzas. Cover one quarter of each of the pizzas with one of the following toppings: mushrooms, ham, artichokes and olives. Season with the oregano, salt and pepper and drizzle with the olive oil. Bake for about 20 minutes.

Pizza alla napoletana
Neapolitan Pizza

1 pizza dough
(see recipe on page 13)
800 g/1 lb 12 oz tomatoes
200 g/7 oz mozzarella
8 anchovies in oil
2 tsp dried oregano
4 tbsp olive oil, plus extra
to grease the pan
flour for dusting
salt and pepper

Preheat the oven to 225°C/435°F/gas mark 7 and grease four round pizza pans with olive oil. Peel and quarter the tomatoes, remove the seeds, and cut into small dice. Thinly slice the mozzarella. Finely chop the anchovies.

Divide the dough into four equal portions and roll them into circles on a floured surface. Place the circles of dough on the pizza pans. Top the dough with the tomatoes, mozzarella and anchovies. Season with the oregano, salt and pepper. Drizzle with the olive oil and bake for about 20 minutes.

Pizza con carciofi
Pizza with Artichokes

1 pizza dough
(see recipe on page 13)
400 g/14 oz artichoke hearts in oil
200 g/7 oz mozzarella
4 tbsp olive oil,
plus extra for greasing
flour for dusting
8 mild chillies in oil
4 garlic cloves, finely chopped
2 tbsp finely chopped parsley
salt and pepper

Preheat the oven to 225°C/435°F/gas mark 7 and grease four round pizza pans with a little olive oil.

Slice the artichoke hearts lengthways and finely dice the mozzarella.

Divide the dough into four equal portions and roll them into circles on a floured surface. Place the circles of dough on the pizza pans. Distribute the artichokes and peppers on top. Sprinkle with garlic and half the parsley. Season with salt and pepper and drizzle on the olive oil. Put the mozzarella on top of the pizzas and bake for about 20 minutes. Sprinkle with the remaining parsley before serving.

Sardenaira
Onion Pizza

1 pizza dough
(see recipe on page 13)
500 g/1 lb 2 oz onions
4 garlic cloves
6 tbsp olive oil,
plus extra for greasing
2 tbsp finely chopped fresh oregano
400 g/14 oz canned diced tomatoes
50 g/1¾ oz salted anchovies
100 g/3½ oz black olives,
stoned and halved
flour for dusting
salt and pepper

Preheat the oven to 225°C/435°F/gas mark 7 and grease four round pizza pans with a little olive oil.

Slice the onions into very fine rings and finely slice the garlic. Heat 4 tablespoons of the olive oil in a deep frying pan and fry the onions and garlic. Stir in the oregano. Remove from the heat and cool slightly.

Divide the dough into four equal portions and roll them into circles on a floured surface. Place the circles of dough on the pizza pans. Top the dough with the onions and tomatoes. Season with salt and pepper.

Rinse the anchovies in cold water, then drain. Distribute the anchovies and olives on the pizzas and drizzle with the remaining olive oil. Bake for about 20 minutes.

Sfinciuni
Sicilian Pizza

1 pizza dough
(see recipe on page 13)
75 ml/2½ fl oz olive oil,
plus extra for greasing
1 small onion, finely chopped
800 g/1 lb 12 oz canned diced tomatoes
300 g/11 oz salted sprats (sardines)
150 g/5 oz caciocavallo cheese (cascaval)
2 tbsp breadcrumbs
flour for dusting
salt and pepper

Preheat the oven to 175°C/350°F/gas mark 4 and grease a springform cake tin (26 cm/10 inches in diameter) with olive oil.

Heat 2 tablespoons of the olive oil and sauté the onions. Add the tomatoes, season with salt and pepper, and leave the sauce to thicken for about 20 minutes.

Rinse the sprats under running cold water and pat dry. Remove the heads and bone the fish. Finely dice the cheese.

Roll out the pizza dough on a floured surface and place it in the springform tin, pressing the dough about 5 cm/2 inches up the side. Brush it with half of the tomato sauce, cover with half of the sprats and add half of the cheese. Then bake for 20 minutes.

Remove the pizza from the oven and top it with the remaining tomato sauce, cheese and sprats. Sprinkle with the breadcrumbs and drizzle on the remaining olive oil. Bake for another 10 minutes.

Pizza con carciofi

Bread

Senza il pane tutto divento orfano. This Italian proverb says, 'Without bread, everyone is an orphan.' A basket of bread – or at least a jar of thin *grissini* (breadsticks) – is an integral part of every Italian table. It is mainly white bread, which is eaten practically around the clock, and in substantial quantities, or so it would seem to foreigners. But appearances can be deceiving. Although it is true that some form of bread must accompany a meal, Italians consume no more bread than do the French, Germans or Spanish. Italians eat mainly white bread, and it comes in every imaginable shape and size. That is probably because white bread used to be reserved for people with higher incomes, while the poor had to settle for darker breads made from maize, rye and chestnut flours. Today, it is just the opposite, although wheat is still the most important grain for bread-making.

Bread, in whatever form, has been a staple food in Italy since antiquity. Even in Roman times, the baker's craft was a major industry. In 100 BCE, there were some 258 bakeries and one baking school in Rome. The Roman emperors also recognized early on that the population could be kept happy with *panem et circenses* (bread and circuses), at least for a while.

'The ratio of bread to drink should be two to one, of bread to eggs one-and-a-half to one, of bread to meat three to one, and of bread to moist fish, green vegetables and fruit, four to one.' Fifteenth-century philosopher Marsilio Ficino established this principle for the ideal consumption of bread in his pamphlet entitled *De longa vita* ('On Long Life'). In the Renaissance, bread was handed out with each course at the feast tables of the Medici family, as well as at the more modest repasts eaten in Leonardo da Vinci's workshops. And according to legend, Michelangelo is said to have nourished himself on bread alone when he worked.

One of the oldest types of bread is *pane di padula*, which is still baked today in the province of Salerno, and is made from a mixture of durum semolina and soft wheat flour. The tops of the round loaves are engraved with squares, and thus resemble the breads depicted on mosaics found in Pompeii. The distinctive bread of the Basilicata region, *pane di matera*, also has a long tradition. Even the Roman poet Horace praised its tasty dough and beguiling scent, for *pane di matera* is made from twice-ground durum semolina and baked in wooden ovens.

Bread is an important staple food throughout Italy, and it is served with every meal. White bread, in particular, is available in every shape and size imaginable. Each region has its own bread recipes and specialities.

The Significance of Bread

Bread is the symbol of life and occupies a central place not only in Christendom. Even in ancient times, it was a symbol of fertility and was offered to the gods during religious ceremonies. Grain symbolized the fertility of the soil, and the bread baked on hot stones was considered sacred.

In the first centuries of Christianity, loaves of bread were very large and ring-shaped. Only from the eleventh century onwards did loaves became smaller and round. In the mid-thirteenth century, eucharistic bread was converted into the Host, which was initially made from the finest wheat and baked only by priests on special grills.

To this day, special breads are baked for certain religious celebrations in Italy. In Basilicata, a ring-shaped bread flavoured with lard and fennel seeds is prepared for the Feast of the Immaculate Conception on 8 December. On Corpus Christi, people in Calabria bake a ring-shaped wholemeal bread that can be hung over people's arms during their procession. And in many regions, ritual speciality breads appear on the table at Easter, on the Feast of Saint Nicholas (6 December) and on the Feast of Saint Lucia (13 December).

Italians rarely throw bread away, not least due to its great symbolic importance. Bread crusts can be used to thicken soups, breadcrumbs to thicken sauces and hardened leftover bread is added to soups and salads.

Regional Breads

On any trip through Italy, you will soon discover that every region has its own speciality breads that are made from different ingredients. There are over 200 types of Italian bread, which, given the diversity of shapes and local names, proudly add up to 1,500 different kinds of bread and rolls.

Depending on the flour used, they can be categorized as regular white bread, rye bread, granary bread or speciality bread made from mixed flours. In the Abruzzo region, the traditional *pane cappelli* is still made from durum wheat semolina. In the province of Teramo, a speciality is *parruozzo*, a soft cornbread that is eaten with boiled vegetables. And the Sicilian province of Messina is home to *pane a birra*, made with brewer's yeast, then plaited and strewn with sesame seeds.

Carta da musica

For centuries, the island of Sardinia has been home to a very special kind of bread, *pane carasau* or *carta da musica* (literally, 'music paper'), so called because it is as thin as paper. The wafer-thin flatbreads are baked and dried. They have a very long shelf life, and were once a basic staple food for shepherds. *Carasau* is heated over the fire or in the oven and then eaten with a drop of olive oil and some salt. It is also softened in milk, then filled with cheese or vegetables and rolled up. A particular speciality is Sardinian shepherd soup, *zuppa dei pastori galluresi*, a hearty lamb soup with fresh vegetables. The ingredients are layered with *carasau* in a heavy casserole, sprinkled with cheese and then oven-grilled. The preparation is particularly elaborate, so this soup tends to be served primarily on special occasions.

Panino classico

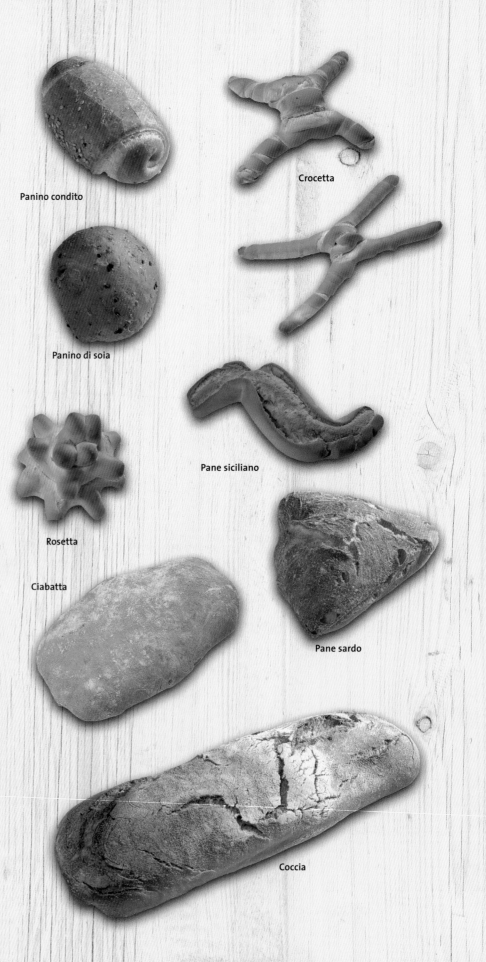

Panino condito

Crocetta

Panino di soia

Pane siciliano

Rosetta

Ciabatta

Pane sardo

Coccia

Frisella casareccia

Frustina

Michetta

Marsigliese

Frisella integrale

Tarallo sugna e pepe

Miciarella

Sfilatino

Pane napoletano

Panello canole

Baking Bread

The ingredients for good bread have remained the same for millennia: flour, water, yeast and usually a little salt. In addition to these fundamental components, the approximately 35,000 Italian bakers are allowed to enrich their breads with many other natural ingredients: butter, olive oil, lard, milk, grape must, grapes, raisins, figs, olives, nuts, almonds, rosemary, aniseed, oregano, caraway, sesame, flaxseed, malt, sucrose or dextrose, pumpkin and honey are all permitted. Thus, in addition to traditional classic breads, there are delicious *panini dolci*, sweet breads with raisins (*all'u vetta pane*), almond bread (*pane con le mandorle*) and nut bread (*pane con le noci*), to name just a few.

Pane casalingo alle olive
Home-made Olive Bread

Ingredients for 3 small loaves:
500 g/1 lb 2 oz plain flour, plus extra for dusting
1 sachet easy-blend dried yeast
1 tsp salt
1 pinch sugar
300 ml/11 fl oz lukewarm water
250 g/9 oz chard, chopped
100 g/3½ oz black olives, stoned and chopped
2 tbsp olive oil, plus extra for greasing

Sift the flour into a bowl and make a hollow in the middle. Place the yeast, salt and sugar in the hollow, then add the water. Knead the mixture into a smooth, silky dough. Leave it to rise, covered, for about 1 hour or until it has doubled in size.

Grease a baking tray with olive oil and preheat the oven to 220°C/430°F/gas mark 7. Knead the chard and olives into the dough, then divide it into thirds. Form each third into a rounded rectangular loaf and place on a greased baking tray. Cover the loaves with a flour-dusted tea towel and leave them to rise again for 1 hour.

Brush the loaves with olive oil and bake for 20 to 25 minutes. Cool thoroughly on a metal rack.

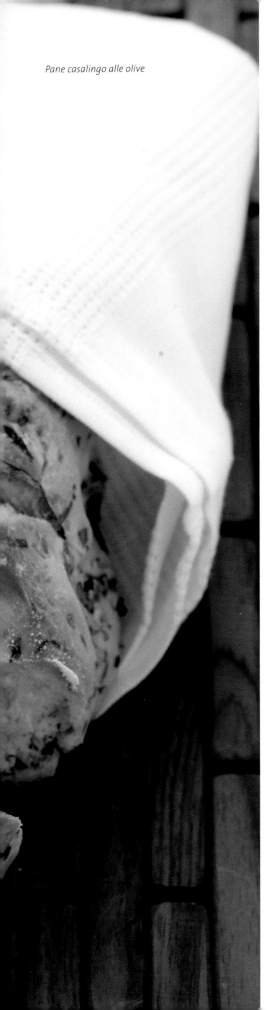

Pane casalingo alle olive

Taralli
Bread Rings

40 g/1½ oz compressed fresh yeast or 2 sachets easy-blend dried yeast
1 pinch sugar
500 g/1 lb 2 oz flour, plus extra for dusting
1 tsp salt
1 tsp fennel seeds, crushed
120 g/4 oz soft lard
olive oil

Crumble the yeast into 250 ml/9 fl oz luke-warm water and dissolve it along with the sugar. Stir in 4 tablespoons of the flour, cover and leave the resulting sponge to prove in a warm place for 15 minutes.

Sift the remaining flour into a bowl, make a hollow in the centre, and pour the sponge into it. Add the salt, fennel seeds and lard and knead everything into a smooth, silky dough. Shape it into a ball, cover, and leave in a warm spot to rise for 1 hour or until it has doubled in volume.

Vigorously knead the dough. On a floured surface, form it into a roll and cut it into 10 equal pieces. Roll each piece into a thin coil and shape into a ring. Place the dough rings on a baking tray covered with baking paper, brush with a little olive oil, cover with a tea towel and leave them to rise for 1 hour. Preheat the oven to 160°C/320°F/gas mark 3. Bake the bread rings for 50 to 60 minutes, then cool completely on a metal rack.

The raw materials for all white breads and rolls are wheat flour, yeast, water and usually a little salt.

First, a sponge is made from a portion of the flour, crumbled yeast and lukewarm water.

Once the sponge has risen, it is thoroughly kneaded with the remaining flour and other ingredients.

Shaped into a ball, the dough is covered and set in a warm place to rise until doubled in volume.

Then the dough is vigorously pulled and kneaded by hand again for a few minutes.

Finally, the finished dough is formed into a loaf and left to rise a second time before baking.

Focaccia alla salvia

Focaccia

Focaccia is a very popular flatbread in Liguria. When baked to perfection, it is soft inside and crisp outside. In earlier times, it used to be eaten as a meal in itself with fresh figs. Today it is available around the clock, an indispensable part of breakfast, snack time, or a savoury bite to eat with aperitifs. In Genoa and the surrounding area, numerous *panetterie* and *focaccerie* offer this delicious flatbread from the early hours of the morning onwards. And many locals eat the bread directly from the bag while walking down the street.

The medieval town of Recco in Liguria is considered the birthplace of cheese focaccia. Long ago, a certain Mr Manuelina Maggio is supposed to have baked this special flatbread for the first time. His recipe: a simple yeast dough with oil produced in the Ligurian Riviera, filled with *stracchino*, the rich, soft cheese native to this region.

Since 1976, the gastronomic consortium of Recco has organized events featuring *focaccia col formaggio*, which has been a protected trademark since 1995. Each year on the fourth Sunday in May, Recco celebrates the Focaccia Festival, called the *Sagra della focaccia*. Throughout the day bakers hand out their delicious flatbread free of charge.

Focaccia alla salvia
Focaccia with Sage

40 g/1½ oz compressed fresh yeast or 2 sachets easy-blend dried yeast
1 pinch sugar
400 g/14 oz flour, plus extra for dusting
1 tsp salt
125 ml/4 fl oz olive oil, plus extra for greasing
12 fresh sage leaves, finely chopped
2 tbsp coarse sea salt

Crumble the yeast into 250 ml/9 fl oz lukewarm water and dissolve it along with the sugar. Stir in 4 tablespoons of the flour, cover and leave the resulting sponge to prove in a warm place for 15 minutes.

Sift the remaining flour into a bowl, make a hollow in the centre and pour the sponge into it. Add the salt and 3–4 tablespoons of the olive oil and knead into a silky dough. Shape it into a ball, cover and leave it to rise in a warm spot for 1 hour or until doubled in volume.

Grease a baking tray with olive oil and preheat the oven to 250°C/480°F/gas mark 9. Vigorously knead the dough again, working in the sage leaves. On a floured surface, roll out the dough to a thickness of about 2 cm/¾ inch, then place it on the baking tray. Gently press down on the dough with your fingers to form many little indentations. Brush it with the remaining olive oil, scatter sea salt over the top and bake for 20 to 25 minutes. Cut into squares to serve.

Focaccia con cipolle
Focaccia with Onions

40 g/1½ oz compressed fresh yeast or 2 sachets easy-blend dried yeast
1 pinch sugar
400 g/14 oz flour, plus extra for dusting
1 tsp salt
125 ml/4 fl oz olive oil, plus extra for greasing
2 onions, cut into thin rings
100 g/3½ oz black olives, stoned
2–3 garlic cloves, finely chopped
1 tbsp coarse sea salt
2 tsp crushed peppercorns

Crumble the yeast into 250 ml/9 fl oz lukewarm water and dissolve it along with the sugar. Stir in 4 tablespoons of the flour, cover and leave the resulting sponge to prove in a warm place for 15 minutes.

Sift the remaining flour into a bowl, make a hollow in the centre and pour the sponge into it. Add the salt and 3–4 tablespoons of olive oil and knead into a silky dough. Shape it into a ball, cover and leave to rise for 1 hour or until doubled in volume.

Grease a baking tray with olive oil and preheat the oven to 250°C/480°F/gas mark 9. Vigorously knead the dough. On a floured surface, roll it out to a thickness of about 2 cm/¾ inch, then place on the baking tray and prick with a fork. Cover with the onions and olives and sprinkle with garlic. Drizzle on the remaining olive oil, season with sea salt and pepper, and bake for about 20 minutes.

To make focaccia dough, first dissolve the yeast in lukewarm water along with a little sugar.

Stir in a small amount of flour, cover and leave the sponge to rise in a warm, draught-free spot.

Then knead the sponge with the other ingredients by hand or in a food processor.

Put the dough in a bowl, cover it and leave it to rise until it has doubled in volume.

On a floured surface, roll out the dough into an oval about 2 cm (¾ inch) thick.

Place it on a greased baking tray and cover with onion rings and olives.

Grissini

*40 g/1½ oz compressed fresh yeast or
2 sachets easy-blend dried yeast*

1 pinch sugar

400 g/14 oz flour, plus extra for dusting

1 tsp salt

3 tbsp olive oil

Crumble or sprinkle the yeast in 250 ml/ 9 fl oz lukewarm water and dissolve it with the sugar. Stir in 4 tablespoons of the flour, cover, and leave the resulting sponge in a warm place to prove for 15 minutes.

Sift the remaining flour into a bowl, make a hollow in the middle and pour the sponge into it. Knead into a silky dough, along with the salt and olive oil. Form the dough into a ball, cover and set it aside for 1 hour, or until it has doubled in volume.

Cover two baking trays with baking paper and preheat the oven to 200°C/390°F/ gas mark 6. Knead the dough vigorously, then divide it into about 30 equal portions. Roll out each piece on a floured surface into thin sticks about 30 cm/12 inches long. Place the sticks of dough next to each other on a baking tray and bake for about 15 minutes or until golden brown. Halfway through the baking time, brush the grissini with water. Leave the breadsticks on the trays to cool.

Crostini, Bruschetta and Fettunta

Crostini, at least according to the residents of Florence, are distinctly Florentine appetizers, and there are countless varieties of them. Nonetheless, they are very popular in southern Italy as well. Each and every household, trattoria and restaurant has a particular house recipe for the topping, which is spread on thick slices of white toast, and differs only slightly in the combination of ingredients and accompanying herbs.

In any event, it is an indisputable fact that crostini are just plain good food. In Tuscany, the classic topping is made from chicken or wild game liver pâté, while in Campania they use juicy, ripe tomatoes. Olive and artichoke pastes are preferred in Apulia, and a fine truffle cream in Piedmont. But there are no limits to a cook's fantasy. Tuscan country bread has not been obligatory for some time now: baguette, focaccia, and corn and rye breads are also used to make crostini.

Traditional Tuscan cuisine is country style. The distinctive regional products from this area for centuries have been olive oil and unsalted white bread. There have been many attempts to explain why, even today, salt is not used in baking bread here. Culinary historians believe it is due to the Tuscan preference for highly spiced ham and salami, as well as the intense flavours of the foods often eaten. Bread, therefore, is simply meant to highlight the quality of the slightly piquant olive oil or the unique flavours of the famous chicken liver pâté and aromatic pastes, rather than to mask them.

When the season for pressing olives begins in late autumn, festive celebrations are held in many little villages to taste the new oil. When it comes straight out of the oil press, it has a sharp flavour that develops best on toast. As far back as ancient Rome, the senate distributed flatbreads dipped in olive oil to the people on important feast days in December and January. Bruschetta – or *fettunta*, as it is called in Tuscany – still tastes best at this time of year.

To this day, saltless Tuscan country bread is still made exclusively from flour and water and baked in wood-burning ovens.

Crostini con erbe e pomodori
Crostini with Herbs and Tomatoes

6 plum tomatoes
1 small bunch basil
2 garlic cloves, minced
3 tbsp olive oil
1 tbsp finely chopped parsley
½ tsp finely chopped oregano
12 small slices Tuscan white bread (or ciabatta)
salt
freshly ground pepper

Skin the tomatoes, quarter them, core and cut into small dice. Rinse the basil, shake it dry and cut the leaves into fine strips. Combine the tomatoes with the garlic, olive oil, salt, pepper and herbs, and allow to stand briefly.

Toast, grill or oven-bake the slices of bread on both sides until golden brown. Top each slice with some of the tomato mixture.

Bruschetta
Bruschetta with Garlic and Oil

4 slices Tuscan country bread
2 garlic cloves
4 tbsp olive oil
salt
freshly ground pepper

Toast, grill or oven-bake the slices of bread on both sides until golden brown.

Cut the garlic in half. Rub each slice with half a clove of garlic and drizzle with 1 tablespoon of the olive oil. Season to taste with salt and pepper.

Among the Italian antipasti there are countless varieties of crostini (opposite).

Crostini neri
Crostini with Olive Paste

200 g/7 oz black olives, stoned

3 anchovy fillets in oil

1 tbsp capers

3–4 tbsp olive oil

12 small slices Tuscan white bread (or ciabatta)

12 basil leaves

salt

cayenne pepper

Roughly chop the olives and anchovy fillets. Then purée them together with the capers and as much olive oil as needed to make a thick paste. Season to taste with salt and cayenne pepper.

Toast, grill or oven-bake the slices of bread on both sides until golden brown. Spread each slice with olive paste and garnish with a basil leaf.

Crostini al pomodoro
Crostini with Tomatoes

12 small slices Tuscan white bread (or ciabatta)

2 garlic cloves

2–3 tbsp olive oil

4 small beef tomatoes, sliced

50 g/1¾ oz Parmesan (whole piece, not grated)

salt

freshly ground pepper

a few basil leaves

Toast, grill or oven-bake the slices of bread on both sides until golden brown. Peel the garlic cloves and cut them in half. Rub the toast with garlic and drizzle with the olive oil. Top each piece with tomato slices, season with salt and pepper, and finely slice the Parmesan over the tomatoes.

Cut the basil into fine strips and garnish the crostini with them.

Crostini alla toscana
Crostini with Chicken Liver Pâté

200 g/7 oz chicken liver

2 tbsp olive oil

1 shallot, finely chopped

100 ml/3½ fl oz Vin Santo

1 tbsp finely chopped thyme

12 small slices of Tuscan white bread (or ciabatta)

salt

freshly ground pepper

Rinse and dry the chicken livers, remove the membranes, then chop into small pieces.

Heat the olive oil and sauté the shallot in it until translucent. Add the livers and sauté while stirring. Deglaze with the wine, add the thyme and cook until the wine has nearly evaporated. Remove from the heat, cool slightly, then purée. Season the chicken liver pâté with salt and pepper.

Toast, grill or oven-bake the slices of bread on both sides until golden brown. Cool slightly, then spread with pâté and serve immediately.

PASTA

Pasta

Even today, it is not clear who actually invented the noodle. It is likely that any culture that had mastered the art of baking bread would have also made noodle-like foods from flour and water. But in no other country does *pasta* (literally, 'dough') have such significance as in Italy. Statistically speaking, every Italian enjoys an average of 27 kg (60 lb) of pasta per year. Italians devote more time and attention to it than to any other foodstuff, and no other product in the world better represents a country's cuisine. Pasta combines all the virtues of the Italian kitchen. It is made from simple, but very good ingredients and cooked with dedication, ingenuity and love.

Archaeologists have found the earliest references to the preparation of pasta in Etruscan hillside tombs dating from the fourth century BCE. Reliefs on the gravestones included equipment for making noodles as well as illustrations of flour sacks, pastry boards, pastry tongs, rolling pins and pasta cutters. Many people believe this was the birthplace of pasta.

A major contribution to the further development of pasta was made more than a thousand years later by the Arabs, who 'invented' the drying of fresh noodles and the production of tube-shaped pastas. When they conquered Sicily in the ninth century, they brought this technique with them to the island. The Arabs also introduced new and highly sophisticated forms of irrigation. So it was that grain cultivation flourished in grand style on the once-dry Sicilian soil.

The earliest surviving pasta recipes date back to the Renaissance. In the fifteenth century, Maestro Martino da Como, the famous personal chef to the patriarch of Aquileia, described several ways of making pasta in his *Libro de Arte Coquinaria* ('Book of Culinary Arts'). The cookbook was not written in Latin, as had been the custom heretofore, but rather in colloquial Italian. It contains, among other things, recipes for 'noodles made from the finest flour, egg white and rose water' that were as thin as straw, rolled by hand and dried in the sun. Another recipe describes how to make *con siciliani*, for which the dough is wrapped around a small metal rod so that the noodles remain hollow inside.

Pasta was not a staple at that time, but rather a luxury food for the well-to-do. Pasta cost three times as much as bread and thus was reserved for the privileged classes: refined with sugar and spices (which were also expensive imported goods), it was prepared according to recipes that sound like they would take some getting used to nowadays. Although tomatoes are inextricably linked to pasta in most people's

As recently as one hundred years ago in Naples, noodles were hung in long strands on wooden poles in the open air to dry.

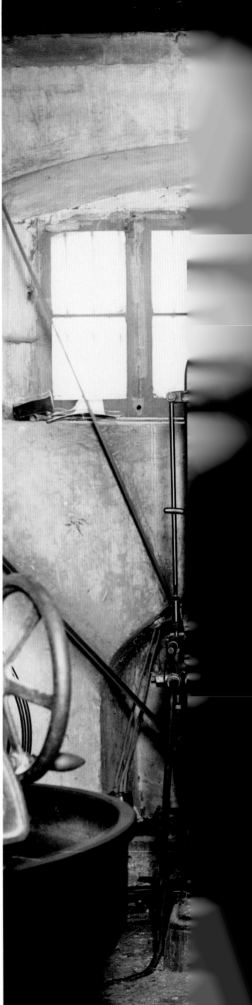

minds today, they were still unknown in Europe at that time.

But pasta's triumphal march was unstoppable. In the eighteenth century, it was poised to overcome class barriers. Naples was the centre of the pasta movement. Not only did durum wheat flourish in the province of Campania; its climate, characterized by sunshine, gentle breezes around the Gulf of Naples and hot winds from Vesuvius, was ideally suited for the production of dried noodles. Here, pasta could dry slowly enough so that it did not become brittle, yet fast enough to avoid becoming mouldy. By the end of the eighteenth century, hundreds of pasta shops lined the streets of Naples. The pasta was cooked at open stalls over charcoal fires, and people ate it on the spot with their fingers.

Then politics entered the picture: the great Italian freedom fighter Giuseppe Garibaldi, who wanted to free Italy from foreign rule, supposedly liberated Naples with the battle cry, 'It will be macaroni, I swear to you, that will unite Italy.'

At the beginning of the 20th century, pasta dough was pressed into long spaghetti or macaroni and cut by hand using machines like this (left).

In the past, pasta was cooked and sold by street vendors and eaten right on the spot, with the fingers, while standing (below).

Pasta 35

Making Pasta

Pasta is made from ground durum wheat and water. Depending on the region, eggs may also be added. It is based on semolina, a ground meal that is somewhat more coarse-grained than flour. Producing good pasta begins with the selection of the right kind of durum wheat. Among connoisseurs, Capelli durum wheat is considered the best. This variety originated in the 1920s and is regarded as the forbearer of many of today's durum wheats.

In addition to the major, world-famous Italian pasta producers, there are still a number of small artisan *pastifici* (pasta manufacturers) such as the Lucchese and Latini enterprises, which are still devoted to producing pasta according to the old, traditional methods. With these pastas, the strong flavour of the grain is in the foreground.

The wheat grains are separated from the outer layers during milling. Some producers grind only the innermost part of the grain into coarse semolina; others mill the whole grain, including the wheat germ. The semolina is kneaded with cold water.

The dough is prepared slowly and gently, so that the gluten in the semolina has sufficient time to develop, which is what will later give the pasta its firm consistency. Whereas home cooks must repeatedly knead the pasta dough, press it flat, pound it and then press it again until it becomes smooth and elastic, in the factory any air that interferes with the pasta dough is removed inside a vacuum chamber in order to make it malleable.

Factory-made dough is then placed in a press and squeezed through nozzles or moulds under high pressure to shape it into the various types of pasta, or it is rolled flat and cut into ribbons of different thicknesses. In handmade artisan factories, the noodles are drawn through bronze dies. Bronze has a rough surface and passes on this texture to the pasta. Teflon-coated dies are used in the larger factories, resulting in noodles with a very smooth surface. However, these noodles don't absorb the sauce nearly as well as handmade, slightly porous pasta.

The final stage is drying, a process in which the pasta is evenly dehydrated from the inside out. If this occurs too quickly, the noodles become brittle. They lose not only some of their nutritive value and taste, but also their appetizing appearance when they are eventually cooked. The gentlest

In Italy there are more than 600 different types, shapes and sizes of pasta. Imaginative new creations are introduced all the time.

drying takes place at 35–50°C (95–120°F), depending on the type of pasta, and lasts between twelve and forty-eight hours.

In old granite flour mills, the durum wheat grain is ground into a coarse meal, semolina, the basis for good, handmade artisan pasta (right).

In a factory, the dough is rolled out into large, thin sheets, then cut into ribbon-style pasta.

Durum Wheat

Pasta is made from semolina, which is produced from coarsely ground durum wheat. Golden durum wheat has a higher gluten content and a different structure than soft wheat, which is better suited for baking. The higher gluten content makes pasta dough elastic and malleable, yet with a firm consistency, which ensures that the pasta retains its shape during cooking.

As early as 1574, the Genoese guild of pasta producers decreed in their bylaws that only durum wheat, *semola*, and water were to be used for their pasta. According to present-day Italian food law, authentic pasta must still be made from durum wheat semolina. When that is the case, the label reads '*pasta di semola di grano duro*'.

After foreign competitors had successfully marketed egg noodles with Italian names and shapes, the Italians themselves started to produce *pasta all'uovo*. They can be purchased fresh or dried, mainly as stuffed or ribbon-style pasta.

Wheat grain

Italian flour

Pasta with Tradition

In Italy there are still a number of *pastifici* (pasta producers) whose pasta is made in traditional, artisan style from high-quality durum wheat and fresh spring water, drawn by old machines with bronze dies and gently dried at a low temperature for up to fifty hours. These producers include Cavalier Giuseppe Cocco from Abruzzo, Leonardo Saltarelli (Perugia), the Martelli family from Lari in the province of Pisa, Pastificio Fabbri from Strada in Chianti, Pasta Lucchese (Tuscany), La Fabbrica della Pasta Gragnano near Naples and the Latini family (the Marche), who, in addition to growing the durum wheat for their pasta, also cultivate the old Senatore Capelli strain of wheat.

The great pasta manufacturer De Cecco started over 120 years ago with a stone mill in Fara San Martino, where the firm produced 'the best flour in the region'. A pasta factory was built next door in which the noodles were not dried in the sun but, for the first time, in a low temperature drying facility. This better preserved the texture of the starch, and the fleeting aromatic compounds could no longer escape.

Home-made Pasta

For Italian home cooks, starting with fresh ingredients is a given, so naturally *pasta fresca* (fresh pasta) is still made at home today. Generally, a distinction is made between *pasta liscia* (smooth and flat such as ribbon noodles) and *pasta ripiena* (shapes that are stuffed). Golden ribbon noodles were allegedly invented in 1503 by a cook from Bologna, who was inspired by Lucrezia Borgia's long blond curls.

As is the case with the use of butter versus olive oil for cooking, there is a kind of border drawn through the country with regard to their use in pasta dough. In Emilia-Romagna, noodle dough is traditionally made with many eggs and flour, but without any water or salt. In Piedmont, cooks reckon on using eight fresh eggs or three whole eggs and nine egg yolks per kilogram of fine wheat flour, known in Britain as Italian flour. Here and there, similar recipes can also be found in Abruzzo, the Marche, Lazio, Umbria and Tuscany. In Liguria and Veneto, on the other hand, the dough contains fewer eggs but more flour, and olive oil is sometimes added. In the southern part of Italy, only durum wheat semolina and water belong in classic pasta dough.

Pasta fatta in casa (pasta fresca)
Fresh Home-made Pasta

400 g/14 oz Italian flour, plus extra for dusting

1 pinch salt
1 egg
2 tbsp olive oil

Sift the flour on to a work surface and press a hollow in the centre. Stir together 8 tablespoons of water with the salt, egg and olive oil and pour the mixture into the hollow. Stir everything together until it forms a smooth, supple dough. Shape the dough into a ball and leave it to rest under a damp cloth for 40 minutes.

Separate the dough into small portions. Using a pasta machine, roll out to the desired thickness according to the manufacturer's instructions.

Cut the dough sheets to the desired width with the appropriate attachment. Roll the noodles into loose nests with a fork, place them side by side on a board or baking tray and leave to dry a little.

For egg noodle dough, first sift the flour on to a work surface, press a hollow in the centre, then add eggs, salt, water and olive oil.

With a wooden spoon, stir in part of the flour from the edge towards the centre. Then knead all the ingredients into a silky, smooth dough by hand.

Leave the dough to rest beneath a damp cloth for 40 minutes. After that, use a rolling pin to roll it out into the thinnest possible rectangular sheet.

Pasta rossa
Red Pasta

400 g/14 oz Italian flour,
plus extra for dusting

1 pinch salt

3 tbsp tomato purée

1 tbsp olive oil

3 eggs

Sift the flour on to a work surface and press a hollow in the centre. Stir together the salt, tomato purée, olive oil and 1 tablespoon of water and pour into the hollow. Add the eggs and knead everything into a silky, smooth dough for 10 minutes. Add 1–2 tablespoons of water, as needed. Shape the dough into a ball and leave it to rest under a damp cloth for 40 minutes.

Pasta verde
Green Pasta

200 g/7 oz frozen spinach, thawed

1 pinch salt

400 g/14 oz Italian flour,
plus extra for dusting

3 eggs

1 tbsp olive oil

Drain the spinach well, purée it with the salt and steam in a non-stick pan until thickened. Remove from the heat and set aside to cool.

Sift the flour on to a work surface and press a hollow in the centre. Place the eggs, olive oil and puréed spinach in the hollow and knead everything into a silky, smooth dough. Add 1–2 tablespoons of water, as needed. Shape the dough into a ball and leave it to rest under a damp cloth for 40 minutes.

Pasta nera
Black Pasta

400 g/14 oz Italian flour,
plus extra for dusting

1 pinch salt

8 g squid ink
(2 sachets of 0.15-oz)

1 tbsp olive oil

3 eggs

Sift the flour on to the work surface and press a hollow in the centre. Stir together the salt, squid ink, olive oil and 1 tablespoon of water and pour into the hollow. Add the eggs and knead everything into a silky, smooth dough. Add 1–2 tablespoons of water, as needed. Shape the dough into a ball and leave it to rest under a damp cloth for 40 minutes.

For ribbon noodles, dust the sheet of dough with flour and loosely roll it up lengthways. Cut it into thin strips with a large, sharp knife.

Unroll the noodle strands, then roll them up with a fork into small, loose nests and place them side by side on a lightly floured board.

Leave the noodles to dry a little before cooking. The longer the noodles dry, the longer they take to cook. Fully dried, they will keep for weeks.

Pasta al Dente

If a few basic guidelines are followed, cooking pasta to perfection is child's play. The most important one is to prepare and serve the pasta immediately after pouring off the cooking water. That explains why, in Italy, one asks guests who come for a meal, '*Si butta?*' ('To the table?'), which roughly means, 'Should I put the pasta on to cook?'

A pasta kettle should be generously sized and as wide as possible so that the heat is distributed evenly. In general, use 1 litre (1¾ pints) of water and 10 grams (⅓ oz) of salt, preferably sea salt, for every 100 grams (3½ oz) of pasta. Heat the water first, and when the water comes to the boil, add the salt and then the noodles. Stir briefly at this point so that the pasta does not stick together. Cook the pasta for the length of time indicated on the packet, stirring occasionally. Shortly before the end of the cooking time, test for doneness by simply taking a noodle from the pot and splitting it with a fork. If the inside has a white circle or white dots, the pasta needs to cook a little longer. If the pasta has an even colour, it is *al dente*, and ready to eat. Translated literally as 'to the tooth', *al dente* means that the pasta is still firm, and not too soft or mushy. Now the pasta is ready to be drained, mixed with the sauce and served. There is nothing more needed in order to cook pasta perfectly.

In Italy, perfectly cooked spaghetti must be al dente, *literally, 'to the tooth' – soft, yet with a bit of bite.*

Pasta and Sauce

The perfect combination of pasta and sauce – in Italian, *sugo* – is an art in itself. Indeed, it is only with the right sauce that pasta can develop its full flavour.

Of course, the choice of sauce is also a matter of personal taste. Nevertheless, there are a few culinary standards: fresh egg noodles and stuffed pasta harmonize nicely with cream and butter sauces, while dried pasta goes well with olive oil-based sauces. The larger the cavity or surface area of the pasta, the more sauce it can absorb and the richer the sauce may be. Thin pasta should never be overwhelmed by too powerful a sauce. A rule of thumb is: the heavier the sauce, the broader the pasta. Tomato sauce, *sugo al pomodoro*, is a classic. It goes with any pasta, provided it is made from flavourful tomatoes and good olive oil and tastefully rounded off with herbs or vegetables.

Meat sauce, *ragù*, stands a close second. In Italy, there are allegedly as many recipes for it as there are stoves. *Ragù* is ideal for tubular pasta, spaghetti and other ribbon-style noodles.

Fish and seafood sauces are ideally suited for long, thin noodles. *Pesto* can be served with spaghetti or ribbon pasta, and even with stuffed pasta.

Sugo ai carciofi e speck

Salsa al Gorgonzola
Gorgonzola Sauce

1 tbsp butter
100 g/3½ oz Gorgonzola
150 ml/5 fl oz double cream
150 ml/5 fl oz milk
2 sage leaves, finely chopped
salt
freshly ground pepper

Heat the butter, Gorgonzola, double cream and milk in the top of a double boiler, stirring slowly until the cheese is melted. Season the sauce with the sage, and salt and pepper to taste.

Sugo ai carciofi e speck
Artichoke and Bacon Sauce

8 small purple artichokes
4 tbsp lemon juice
4 garlic cloves
150 g/5 oz pancetta
5 tbsp olive oil
250 ml/9 fl oz dry white wine
400 ml/14 fl oz stock
(or according to taste)
salt
freshly ground pepper

Trim the artichokes, shorten the stalks to about 4 cm/1½ inches and peel them. Remove the tough outer leaves as well as the hard thorns from the remaining leaves. Combine the lemon juice and some water in a bowl. Slice the artichokes lengthways and immediately place them in the bowl of lemon water. Leave them to soak a little, then pour off the liquid and pat dry.

Peel the garlic and cut into thin slices. Dice the bacon. Heat the olive oil in a large frying pan and sauté the bacon and artichokes. Add the garlic and fry until golden brown. Deglaze with the wine. Pour in the stock, bring to the boil, and season with salt and pepper. Cover the vegetables and cook on low heat for about 15 minutes until the artichokes are done.

Salsa alla cacciatora
Hunter's Sauce

50 g/1¾ oz dried ceps
4 tbsp olive oil
1 onion, finely chopped
1 garlic clove, finely chopped
50 g/1¾ oz smoked pancetta, diced
1 celery stick, finely diced
50 g/1¾ oz dry-cured
or smoked ham, diced
100 ml/3½ fl oz red wine
1 bay leaf
150 ml/5 fl oz double cream
salt
freshly ground pepper

Soak the ceps in 250 ml/9 fl oz lukewarm water for 30 minutes. Then drain the mushrooms through a fine sieve, retaining the soaking water, and roughly chop the ceps. Heat the olive oil in a deep frying pan. Fry the onion, garlic and pancetta in the oil until the onions are translucent. Add the celery and ham, and season with salt and pepper. Pour in the red wine and reduce.

Add the ceps, soaking water and bay leaf to the pan. Simmer the sauce for 10 minutes. Stir in the cream and leave the sauce to reduce for another 10 minutes. Remove the bay leaf and season the sauce to taste with salt and pepper.

Sugo con le conchiglie
Shellfish Sauce

1 kg/2 lb 4 oz mixed shellfish
1 kg/2 lb 4 oz plum tomatoes
5 tbsp olive oil
1 large onion, finely chopped
2 garlic cloves, finely chopped
2 celery sticks, diced
2 carrots, diced
2 tbsp finely chopped parsley
salt
freshly ground pepper

Thoroughly wash the shellfish, brushing the shells and removing the beards as needed, and discard any shells that are open. Peel the tomatoes, cut them into wedges, remove the seeds, and cut into fine dice. Heat the olive oil in a large saucepan and sauté the onion and garlic until the onion is translucent. Add the celery and carrots and cook briefly. Stir in the shellfish, cover the pan and cook on high heat for about 5 minutes, shaking the pan a few times.

Remove the shellfish from the pot and discard any shells that are still closed. Add the tomatoes to the vegetable mixture, season with salt and pepper and reduce slightly.

Add the shellfish to the tomato sauce and simmer briefly on low heat. Stir in the chopped parsley.

Salsa all'amatriciana
Tomato and Bacon Sauce

150 g/5 oz pancetta
500 g/1 lb 2 oz tomatoes
2 tbsp olive oil
1 small onion, finely chopped
1 fresh red chilli, finely chopped
salt
freshly ground pepper

Chop the pancetta into fine dice. Peel and quarter the tomatoes, remove the seeds, and chop roughly.

Heat the olive oil in a pan and render the pancetta. Add the onion and chilli to the pan and fry until the onions are translucent. Stir in the tomatoes and simmer the sauce for 15 to 20 minutes. Season with salt and pepper to taste.

Sugo con le conchiglie

Ragù alla bolognese
Bolognese Sauce

25 g/1 oz dried ceps
1 tbsp butter
50 g/1¾ oz pancetta, diced
1 small onion, minced
1 garlic clove, minced
2 small carrots, minced
2 celery sticks, minced
300 g/11 oz minced beef
1 pinch sugar
1 tbsp tomato purée
125 ml/4 fl oz red wine
250 g/9 oz canned tomato purée
salt
freshly ground pepper
freshly grated nutmeg

Soak the ceps in 125 ml/4 fl oz lukewarm water for 20 minutes.

Melt the butter in a frying pan and fry the pancetta in it. Add the onion and garlic and fry until the onion is translucent. Stir in the carrots and celery and cook for a few minutes, stirring frequently.

Mix in the mince and brown it, stirring constantly. Season with salt, pepper, nutmeg and a pinch of sugar. Stir in the tomato purée and cook for a minute or two, then add the red wine. Mix in the tomato purée.

Finely slice the ceps and add them to the sauce. Pour the soaking water through a fine sieve into the sauce. Thicken the sauce by cooking it on low heat for 1 hour.

Ragù

Some critics claim that there are as many recipes for *ragù* in Italy as there are stoves on which the meat sauce is cooked. The types of meat, vegetables, spices and herbs certainly do vary by region, and the recipes are modified according to personal preferences and family traditions.

Ragù alla romagnola, made from minced beef, salsiccia, pancetta, carrots, celery, onion, tomatoes and white wine, comes from Piedmont. For *ragù alla napoletana*, pork is cooked in lard. In the Abruzzo region, lamb is stewed in white wine with tomatoes, peppers, garlic and bay leaves. All of these meat sauces have one thing in common: while the older generation, in particular, insists that a genuine *ragù* has to simmer for at least two hours, or better still three hours, the tendency nowadays is to leave the sauce to cook on the hob for a shorter period. This not only saves time, but also maintains the unique flavours of the individual ingredients.

For an authentic Bolognese sauce, first soak dried ceps in lukewarm water.

Then fry the pancetta and finely diced vegetables in olive oil.

The next step is to add the minced beef and brown it until it is crumbly.

Season the mixture with salt, pepper and nutmeg, stir in the tomato purée, and cook it briefly.

Add the finely chopped ceps and pour in the soaking water while straining it through a sieve.

Italian Olive Oils

When it comes to olive oils, about 250 different types of olive trees produce a wide palette of flavours. Broadly speaking, Italy can be divided into four cultivation zones:

Liguria, Sardinia and the Coastal Zones of Tuscany Due to the particular marine climate, the oils from here have a rather light and delicate flavour.

Central Italy The oils from Tuscany and Umbria are, above all, highly aromatic, especially when freshly pressed, and have a strong 'bite' in the aftertaste.

Southern Italy These are very pungent oils with an intense, almost 'fatty' olive flavour that results from the hot climate.

Sicily Various microclimates on the island generate a rich variety of oils, found nowhere else in Italy.

Basil

Basil has been cultivated for over 4,000 years. The ancient Greeks called the intensely aromatic plant 'the royal herb', and treasured not only its powerful fragrance, but also its healing properties. Basil originally came from Asia. Today there are at least sixty varieties of basil, the most familiar of which are small-leaf Greek basil, and sweet or Italian basil, also called *Basilico genovese*. Both of these have a distinctly different flavour than the Asian and African varieties. When used fresh, delicate green basil leaves from the Mediterranean regions have a slightly peppery, spicy-sweet flavour. These sensitive plants need a lot of sun and plentiful moisture. Liguria has nearly ideal climatic conditions for optimal cultivation, as does Piedmont. When using basil in cooking, it should not be cooked with the rest of the ingredients, but instead should be added at the end of the cooking process. Apropos, basil is a symbol of love in Italy.

Pesto alla genovese
Pesto Sauce

2 tbsp pine kernels
3–4 garlic cloves
2 handfuls fresh basil
½ tsp salt
1 tbsp each: grated Parmesan and Pecorino Romano
100 ml/3½ fl oz olive oil

Dry-roast the pine kernels in an ungreased frying pan until golden brown. Cool slightly, then chop them roughly. Peel and roughly chop the garlic as well.

Rinse the basil, dry thoroughly and cut the leaves into strips. Put the pine kernels, garlic, basil and salt in a large mortar and crush everything to a paste.

Work the two cheeses into the paste gradually. Then pour in the olive oil in a thin stream and stir until the sauce has a creamy consistency, adding a little water if needed.

Finely chopped basil, pine kernels and garlic form the basis for pesto.

The ingredients are placed in a large mortar made of porcelain, granite or ceramic.

The mixture is ground to a paste and freshly grated cheese is added.

Flavourful olive oil is poured into the paste in a thin stream and blended in.

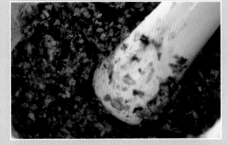

The pesto is mixed into a creamy sauce, with the addition of a little water, as needed.

Many Shapes and Sizes

In Italy, there are more than 600 different types and shapes of pasta on the market. They often differ from one another only minimally in terms of shape, size, diameter and type of dough. Pasta makers go to a great deal of trouble to constantly develop new shapes and fanciful names, and the pasta industry is very creative in this respect. Some of the classic types of pasta have beautiful and onomatopoeic names such as *conchiglie* (shells), *farfalle* (butterflies), *orecchiette* (little ears), *penne* (feather or quill), *ruote* (cartwheel), *strangolapreti* or *strozzapreti* (priest stranglers) and *capelli d'angelo* (angel hair).

In spite of the major pasta producers' marketing efforts, about a dozen standard types still make up over 90 per cent of the pasta market. The rest are regional specialities, new creations that disappear from the market in short order, or pasta created for special occasions such as millennium pasta or pasta in the shape of a tennis racket, produced especially for the world championships.

Pastasciutta

Outside of Italy, *pastasciutta* is one of the most misunderstood pastas, for this is not a matter of a recipe for pasta with meat sauce. *Pastasciutta* (literally, 'dry pasta') describes all kinds of pasta dishes that can be prepared with sauce or cheese, from simple spaghetti with tomato sauce to sophisticated pumpkin tortellini in butter to rich lasagne. Despite the sauce that adorns them, and unlike noodles in stock or soup, in Italian cuisine these pastas are considered 'dry'.

Pastasciutta, like risotto or gnocchi, is served as a first course in restaurants, and it is customarily followed by a meat or fish course. That is why the portions of pasta served are not all that generous. In Italy, it is still not the custom to order *pastasciutta* as a meal in itself. This puts off Italian gastronomes to the same degree as the habit many tourists have of sprinkling cheese over every pasta dish, even if it contains fish or seafood.

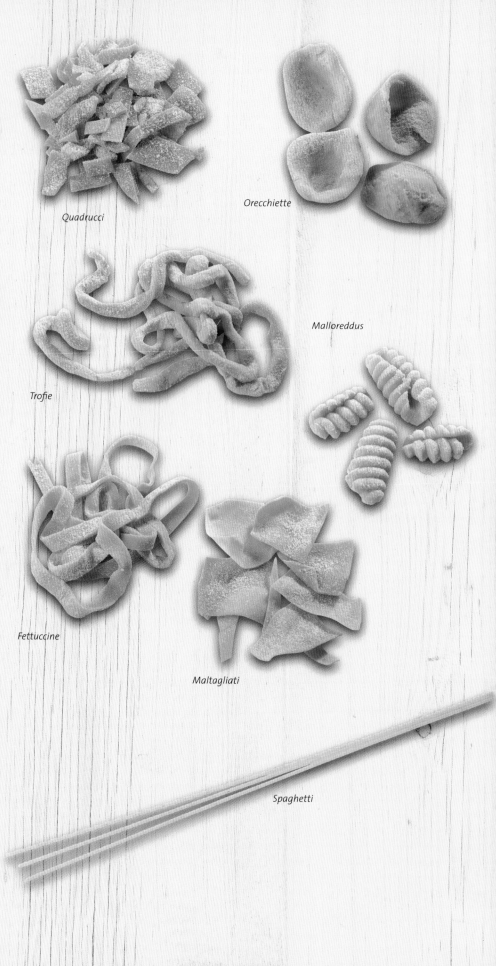

Quadrucci

Orecchiette

Malloreddus

Trofie

Fettuccine

Maltagliati

Spaghetti

Penne

Farfalle

Fusilli

Casareccia al Pomodoro

Cavatellucci

Rigatoni

Tagliatelle

Ruote tricolori

Tagliatelle verdi

Tofarelle

Cannelloni

Lasagne

Fusilli tricolori

Spaghetti & Co.

Spaghetti is just one kind of *pasta lunga*, or long noodle. The name is derived from *spago*, the Italian word for 'cord'. Spaghetti is often considered the quintessential Italian pasta abroad, and it is without question the most famous kind of pasta, but it is not the oldest. As a rule, today spaghetti is produced in factories.

The name *spaghetti* was originally a collective term for all forms of dried, cord-like pasta, regardless of its thickness. Today, the designations are more differentiated. Even so, all *vermicelli*, whether thick or thin, have one thing in common: they are eaten with a fork. It is immaterial if waiters give tourists a spoon to go with the fork, because the proper way to eat spaghetti is by wrapping it around the fork at the edge of one's plate. It is perfectly permissible to lean slightly forwards over your plate while doing so.

Spaghettini, also called *vermicelli* in Naples, is thinner than regular spaghetti. Some popular ways to serve it are with shellfish, seafood or simply *aglio, olio, e peperoncino* – that is, with garlic, olive oil and chillies.

Bucatini are very popular in central Italy. This thicker spaghetti with a hole (*buco*) in the centre goes wonderfully with hearty tomato sauces or rich sauces with bacon.

Linguine (literally, 'tongues') resemble rolled-out, flattened spaghetti. They have a somewhat coarse surface that sauces adhere to especially well.

The Royal Spaghetti Fork

Pasta not only brings happiness, but also fosters creativity. Ferdinand II, for example, king of Naples from 1830 to 1859, was a passionate spaghetti aficionado. Since this pasta could not be eaten with the sharp, three-pronged forks that were used at court in those days, and the king didn't want to eat pasta with his fingers like a commoner, he had his steward make a blunt, four-pronged fork, which is the precursor of today's fork design.

Spaghetti alla Chitarra

Spaghetti alla chitarra, also called *maccheroni alla chitarra*, is spaghetti that is about 2 mm thick with a square cross section. It is produced in Abruzzo using a *chitarra* (literally, 'guitar'), a frame that has thin wires stretched across it. The thinly rolled-out dough is laid on top of the strings, then pressed down on them with a rolling pin. And that is how long, thin pasta is made from the dough.

Spaghetti alla Carbonara

400 g/14 oz spaghetti

4 eggs

4 tbsp double cream

50 g/1¼ oz grated Parmesan

50 g/1¼ oz grated Pecorino Romano

1 tbsp butter

150 g/5 oz pancetta, finely diced

salt

freshly ground pepper

Bring a large saucepan of lightly salted water to the boil. Add the pasta and cook according to packet instructions until al dente.

Meanwhile, stir together the eggs, cream and cheeses in a bowl. Add salt and pepper.

Melt the butter in a large frying pan and fry the pancetta until crisp. Drain the spaghetti and add it to the pan while still dripping wet. Pour the cheese sauce over it. Remove the pan from the stove. Toss the pasta in the sauce until the eggs begin to thicken but are still creamy. Serve on heated plates, sprinkled with freshly ground pepper.

Spaghetti aglio, olio e peperoncino
Spaghetti with Garlic, Oil and Chillies

400 g/14 oz spaghetti
100 ml/3½ fl oz olive oil
4–6 garlic cloves, finely chopped
2–3 dried chilli peppers
2 tbsp finely chopped parsley
salt
freshly ground pepper
75 g/2½ oz grated Parmesan

Bring a large saucepan of lightly salted water to the boil. Add the pasta and cook according to packet instructions until al dente.

In a deep frying pan, heat the olive oil and sauté the garlic and whole chillies in it. As soon as the desired spiciness is reached, remove the chillies from the pan. For a very spicy dish, you can leave the chillies in the garlic oil.

Drain the spaghetti, add it to the deep frying pan while still dripping wet, and mix with the hot garlic oil and parsley. Season with pepper and serve on heated plates with the Parmesan on the side.

Spaghetti al pomodoro
Spaghetti with Tomato Sauce

600 g/1 lb 5 oz tomatoes
4 tbsp olive oil
1 pinch sugar
400 g/14 oz spaghetti
1 tbsp finely chopped basil leaves
salt
freshly ground pepper
75 g/2½ oz grated Parmesan
or pecorino cheese

Peel and quarter the tomatoes, remove the seeds and dice. Then heat the olive oil in a large frying pan and cook the tomatoes. Season with the sugar, salt and pepper, and simmer on low heat for about 20 minutes.

Bring a large saucepan of lightly salted water to the boil. Add the pasta and cook it according to packet instructions until al dente. Drain the spaghetti and combine it with the tomato sauce while still dripping wet. Serve on heated plates sprinkled with basil, with the cheese on the side.

Bucatini alla puttanesca
Bucatini with Tomatoes, Capers and Olives

100 g/3½ oz stoned black olives
5 anchovies in oil
4 tbsp olive oil
2 tbsp tomato purée
800 g/1 lb 12 oz canned peeled tomatoes
60 g/2 oz small capers
salt
freshly ground pepper
400 g/14 oz bucatini pasta

Cut the olives into quarters. Finely chop the anchovies. Heat the olive oil in a frying pan, stir in the tomato purée and cook it briefly. Crush the tomatoes with a fork, then add them to the pan. Stir in the olives, anchovies and capers and simmer the sauce on low heat for 20 minutes. Season to taste with salt and pepper.

Bring a large saucepan of lightly salted water to the boil. Add the pasta and cook according to packet instructions until al dente. Drain the bucatini and mix it into the sauce while still dripping wet. Serve immediately on heated plates.

Favourite Pasta Dishes

Tagliolini al tartufo
Tagliolini with White Truffle

400 g/14 oz tagliolini
100 g/3½ oz butter
1 small white truffle
salt

Bring a large saucepan of lightly salted water to the boil. Add the pasta and cook according to packet instructions until al dente.

Meanwhile, melt the butter, but be careful it does not turn brown.

Clean the truffle with a dry, soft brush. Drain the pasta thoroughly, then distribute it on four plates. Pour the melted butter over each serving. With a truffle grater, finely shave the truffle over the pasta.

Linguine con salsa di pesce
Linguine with Fish Sauce

400 g/14 oz fish fillets such as perch or cod
600 g/1 lb 5 oz tomatoes
1 onion
4 tbsp olive oil
350 g/12 oz linguine
1 tbsp finely chopped parsley
flour for coating
salt
freshly ground pepper
basil leaves to garnish

Wash the fish fillets, pat them dry and coat in flour. Peel and quarter the tomatoes, remove the seeds, and dice. Peel the onion, then cut it in half and slice.

Heat the olive oil in a pan and fry the fish on both sides until golden brown, then remove from the pan and keep warm. Sauté the onions in the oil until translucent, then add the tomatoes. Season with salt and pepper, cover the pan and simmer on low heat for about 10 minutes.

In the meantime, bring a large saucepan of lightly salted water to the boil. Add the pasta and cook according to packet instructions until al dente. Drain the pasta and toss it with the tomato sauce and parsley while the pasta is still dripping wet. Cut the fish into bite-sized pieces and blend into the pasta. Cover and briefly allow the flavours to mingle. Serve on heated plates garnished with basil leaves.

Tagliatelle

As if the numerous types of pasta were not confusing enough, the exact same pasta can also have up to ten different names, depending on the region and manufacturer! Luckily, classic tagliatelle have the same name throughout Italy. Often they are available as both dry and fresh egg noodle products.

Tuscan *pappardelle* are the widest tagliatelle. The linguistic origin of these delicious noodles is anything but genteel. This Tuscan word originally meant 'to fill one's gullet', and it is also used in this sense in Boccaccio's *Decameron*.

One of the most popular kinds of egg noodles, tagliatelle are about 8 mm wide. Their name comes from the Italian verb *tagliare*, 'to cut'. They are usually available rolled into small nests or spirals. They initially came from Bologna, and go perfectly with meat sauces.

In the vicinity of Rome, the somewhat more slender, thicker tagliatelle are called *fettuccine,* or *trenette* in Liguria. They are just as delightful with a flavourful pesto as with cream or butter sauces containing vegetables, fish or seafood.

Tagliarellini are about 4 mm wide. Green and white *tagliarellini* are the basis for the classic pasta dish *paglia e fieno* ('straw and hay').

Tagliolini, the most delicate of egg noodles, are just 1 mm wide and taste best with just a touch of butter and white truffles.

Pappardelle al sugo di lepre
Pappardelle with Rabbit Sauce

4 rabbit legs
4 tbsp olive oil
1 onion, finely diced
1 carrot, diced
1 celery stick, diced
250 ml/9 fl oz red wine
400 g/14 oz pappardelle
salt
freshly ground pepper
1 tbsp finely chopped parsley

Wash the rabbit legs, pat them dry, then vigorously rub them with salt and pepper.

Heat the olive oil in an iron casserole and sauté the diced vegetables in it. Add the rabbit legs and brown on both sides. Deglaze with the wine, cover and stew on low heat for about 40 minutes until the meat is done. Then take the legs out of the sauce. Remove the meat from the bones, cut it into small cubes and put the meat back into the sauce.

Bring a large saucepan of lightly salted water to the boil. Add the pasta and cook until al dente. Mix the pasta into the sauce while still dripping wet. Add salt and pepper to taste. Serve sprinkled with parsley.

Penne all'arrabbiata
Spicy Penne

500 g/1 lb 2 oz tomatoes
2 tbsp olive oil
100 g/3½ oz pancetta, diced
1 onion, finely chopped
2 garlic cloves, finely chopped
2–3 dried red chillies
400 g/14 oz penne rigate
75 g/2½ oz grated Pecorino Romano
salt

Peel and quarter the tomatoes, remove the seeds, and cut into small dice. Heat the olive oil in a deep frying pan and fry the pancetta in it. Add the onion and garlic and fry until the onions are translucent. Then add the diced tomatoes and whole chillies and leave the sauce to simmer on low heat for a while. As soon as it reaches the desired level of spiciness, remove the chillies from the pan.

Bring a large saucepan of lightly salted water to the boil. Add the pasta and cook for half the time stated in the packet instructions, then drain, reserving some of the pasta cooking water.

Mix the penne, 2 tablespoons of the Pecorino Romano and 3–4 tablespoons of pasta water into the tomato sauce and finish cooking the pasta in the sauce, stirring frequently. Serve on heated plates sprinkled with the remaining Pecorino Romano.

Rigatoni all'amatriciana
Rigatoni with Bacon and Onions

3 tomatoes
2 tbsp olive oil
100 g/3½ oz pancetta, diced
2 small white onions, minced
1 small, dried red chilli, minced
salt
350 g/12 oz rigatoni
60 g/2 oz grated Pecorino Romano

Peel and quarter the tomatoes, remove the seeds, and dice. Heat the olive oil in a large frying pan and fry the diced pancetta until crisp, then remove from the pan and keep warm. Sauté the onion and chilli in the bacon fat. Add the tomatoes, salt lightly and simmer for 10 minutes.

In the meantime, bring a large saucepan of lightly salted water to the boil. Add the pasta and cook according to packet instructions until al dente. Drain the water and tip the pasta into a preheated bowl. Combine it thoroughly with the pancetta, tomato sauce and Pecorino Romano. Serve immediately.

Ziti con salsiccia
Ziti with Sausage

250 g/9 oz salsiccia (Italian sausage)
2 yellow peppers
2 tomatoes
2 tbsp olive oil
1 white onion, finely chopped
2 garlic cloves, finely chopped
250 ml/9 fl oz white wine
1 tbsp oregano, finely chopped
350 g/12 oz ziti
salt
freshly ground pepper

Skin and slice the sausage. Cut the peppers in half, remove the cores, and cut into strips. Peel and quarter the tomatoes, remove the seeds, and cut into small dice.

Heat the olive oil in a deep frying pan and sauté the onions and garlic until the onions are translucent. Add the sliced sausage and peppers and continue to cook, stirring. Add the diced tomatoes, pour in the wine, then season with the oregano and pepper to taste. Simmer for 15 to 20 minutes on low heat.

In the meantime, break the pasta into bite-sized pieces. Bring a large saucepan of lightly salted water to the boil. Add the pasta and cook according to packet instructions until al dente. Drain the pasta and combine with the sauce. Cover and leave it to stand for 1 or 2 minutes. Serve on heated plates.

Naples

An old Neapolitan proverb says, 'Three things can ruin a family: sweets, fresh bread and *maccheroni*.' For a long time, pasta made from fine flour was a costly indulgence. People still sing folksongs that are full of longing for a far-away land in which the heavens rain *maccheroni*. Only with the advent of industrial production did pasta become an affordable food for everyday enjoyment.

In Naples, which is still the centre of pasta making today, factory production began in the nineteenth century with the invention of rolling and kneading machines. In those days, almost every packet of pasta was decorated with a view of the Gulf of Naples and a plume of smoke over Mount Vesuvius.

Neapolitans believe that none less than the god Vulcan could have been the first to convert a formless mass of semolina and water into graceful strands of pasta. After this fare had won over the hearts and palates of the gods, Ceres, the goddess of growing plants and motherly love, revealed the secret of pasta making to the Neapolitans, for whom she held a special fondness.

Pipe con rana pescatrice
Pipe with Monkfish

400 g/14 oz monkfish fillets
400 g/14 oz pipe pasta
60 ml/2 fl oz olive oil
1 small white onion, finely chopped
1 garlic clove, finely chopped
1 tbsp chopped capers
1 tbsp finely chopped parsley
salt
freshly ground pepper

Wash the fish, pat it dry and dice. Bring a large saucepan of lightly salted water to the boil. Add the pasta and cook according to packet instructions until al dente.

Meanwhile, heat the olive oil in a deep saucepan and sauté the onion and garlic in it. Add the fish to the pan and fry for 4 minutes, stirring continuously. Season with salt and pepper, then add the capers.

Drain the pasta and combine it with the fish while still dripping wet. Cover the pan and leave it to stand for a minute or two. Add the parsley. Serve the pasta on four heated plates.

Trofie pesto rosso
Trofie with Red Pesto

For the dough:

300 g/11 oz durum wheat flour,
plus extra for dusting
1 tsp white wine vinegar
2 tbsp olive oil
1 pinch salt
3 tbsp semolina

For the pesto:

50 g/1¾ oz pine kernels
2 garlic cloves, chopped
1 fresh red chilli, chopped
150 g/5 oz sun-dried tomatoes in oil
1 tbsp tomato purée
freshly ground pepper
1 tbsp grated Parmesan

Sift the flour into a bowl and make a well in the centre. Pour in about 150 ml/5 fl oz water and the vinegar, olive oil and salt. Knead everything into a smooth, silky dough. Divide the dough into two portions. Roll both of them out thin on a floured work surface and leave it to dry a little. Sprinkle the dough with the semolina and, using a sharp knife or pastry wheel, cut into thin noodles and roll them by hand.

For the pesto, dry-roast the pine kernels in an ungreased frying pan on low heat until golden brown, stirring constantly. Purée the pine kernels, garlic, chilli and tomatoes (including the oil) in a blender. Mix in the tomato purée and as much water as needed to make a smooth paste. Season generously with salt and pepper.

Bring a large saucepan of lightly salted water to the boil. Add the pasta and cook until al dente. Stir the Parmesan and 3 tablespoons of the pasta cooking water into the pesto sauce. Drain the pasta, tip it into a heated bowl, combine with the pesto and serve immediately. Sprinkle with additional Parmesan, if desired.

Orecchiette con broccoli
Orecchiette with Broccoli

500 g/1 lb 2 oz broccoli florets
1 fresh red chilli
4 anchovy fillets in oil
100 ml/3½ fl oz olive oil
4 garlic cloves, finely chopped
25 g/1 oz pine kernels
400 g/14 oz canned peeled tomatoes
300 g/11 oz orecchiette
60 g/2 oz grated Pecorino Romano
salt
freshly ground pepper

Bring a saucepan of salted water to the boil and blanch the broccoli florets for 3 minutes. Drain the broccoli thoroughly, reserving the cooking water.

Halve and core the chilli. Rinse the anchovies under cold running water. Finely chop both. Heat the olive oil in a deep frying pan and fry the chilli, anchovies, garlic and pine kernels. Add the tomatoes, season with salt and pepper, and simmer for 15 minutes.

Meanwhile, bring the broccoli water to the boil once more and cook the orecchiette in it until al dente. Drain the pasta and add it to the tomato sauce while still dripping wet. Blend in the broccoli florets and 2 tablespoons of the Pecorino Romano. Cover the pan and heat for a few minutes on low heat. Sprinkle the remaining cheese on top and serve.

Farfalle con pomodori secchi e basilico
Farfalle with Sun-dried Tomatoes and Basil

30 g/1 oz sun-dried tomatoes
50 g/1¾ oz pine kernels
1 handful fresh basil
2 garlic cloves, chopped
½ tsp salt
100 ml/3½ fl oz olive oil
1 tbsp grated Parmesan
400 g/14 oz farfalle
salt
freshly ground pepper

Pour hot water over the sun-dried tomatoes and soak them for 25 minutes. Then pour off the water, squeeze out the liquid and chop.

Dry-roast the pine kernels in an ungreased frying pan until golden brown. Wash the basil and pat it dry, then pluck off the leaves. Crush half of the pine kernels with the basil leaves, garlic and salt in a large mortar. Gradually work in the olive oil, then add the Parmesan last. Stir the chopped tomatoes into the basil sauce.

Bring a large saucepan of lightly salted water to the boil. Add the pasta and cook according to packet instructions until al dente. Drain the pasta and combine it, still dripping wet, with the basil-tomato sauce in a heated bowl. Serve on warmed plates seasoned with pepper and sprinkled with the remaining pine kernels.

Cut off thin strips from a sheet of pasta dough with a pastry wheel or a knife.

Fully purée the ingredients for the red pesto sauce in a food processor or blender.

Cook the pasta until al dente in plenty of salted water, then drain it and combine with the pesto.

Trofie pesto rosso

Pizzoccheri
Buckwheat Pasta
with Savoy Cabbage

100 g/3½ oz buckwheat flour

100 g/3½ oz wholemeal flour,
plus extra for dusting

1 egg

2 egg yolks

1 tsp salt

3–5 tbsp white wine

250 g/9 oz Savoy cabbage

2 potatoes

100 g/3½ oz butter

2 garlic cloves, finely sliced

6 sage leaves, cut into strips

250 g/9 oz Valtellina Casera cheese, diced

Sift both flours on to a work surface and make a well in the centre. Put the egg, egg yolks, salt and white wine in the hollow and knead everything into a smooth, silky dough. Wrap the dough in a damp cloth and set it aside for 1 hour at room temperature.

On a floured work surface, roll out the dough to a thickness of 5 mm/⅕ inch. Use a pastry wheel to cut out pieces of pasta approximately 5 x 2 cm/2 x ¾ inch. Cut the Savoy cabbage into thin strips and slice the potatoes. Bring a large saucepan of lightly salted water to the boil. Add the cabbage and potatoes and cook for 15 minutes. Then add the pasta and cook for another 10 minutes.

Meanwhile, melt the butter and stir in the garlic and sage. Drain the potatoes, cabbage and pasta and place them in a preheated bowl. Mix in the Valtellina Casera cheese and pour the sage butter over the dish.

Pasta Ripiena, Delicious and Much Loved

Pasta ripiena (stuffed or filled pasta) has captured the fancy and stimulated the creativity of Italian chefs for centuries. Even today, the starting point is pasta dough made with fresh eggs, filled with all sorts of delicious things and shaped into 'pockets', squares, rectangles, triangles, circles, rings, crescents, even 'hats'. *Pasta ripiena* is mainly found in northern and central Italy. This is

The basis of very popular northern and central Italian pasta ripiena is fresh egg noodle dough cut into various shapes and stuffed.

because fresh eggs, a prerequisite for supple, smooth dough that can be easily moulded, used to be a rarity in southern Italy.

Initially, the large selection of *pasta ripiena* can be confusing to non-Italians. Not only their shapes differ almost from city to city, but every region has its own tradition when it comes to the filling, too. In Romagna they use meat, in Emilia, herbs. Stew meat is the custom in Piedmont; herbs, fish or meat in Liguria, and meat or sausage in Tuscany. *Cappelletti*, the smallest stuffed pasta, come from Ferrara and are filled with a turkey mixture. If they are made with pumpkin, they are called *cappellacci*. Large *tortelloni* come from Piacenza and have a ricotta and herb filling. Small *tortellini* from Bologna are stuffed with a mixture of meat, mortadella and ham. *Ravioli* from Modena

contain roast meat, while Parma, the city of *anolini*, uses a meat and vegetable filling. In Piedmont, *agnolotti* are stuffed with meat and cabbage. Ligurian *pansoti* have wild herbs in them and, in the Marche, *cappelletti alla pescarese* have roast pork, cooked capon or turkey filling.

Tortellini

It is said that Venus herself, the goddess of love, served as a model for the beguiling pasta rings called *tortellini*. According to legend, Venus had stopped at a simple inn during a visit to the earth. When the innkeeper brought a refreshment to her room, the naked Venus suddenly stood across from him. Overcome by the perfect shape of her navel, he rushed immediately into the kitchen to replicate it in dough form.

The truth is, tortellini are the culinary emblem of Bologna. In the little lanes of the provincial capital, you can almost look over the shoulders of the tortellini makers while they work. Tortellini are served in a rich broth or with meat ragout. They taste best in one of the typical trattorias between the Piazza Maggiore and the pergolas of the historic old city centre, just a few steps away from the towers of the Asinelli and Garisenda families.

Tortellini are delicious little stuffed 'pasta pockets'. They are traditionally served with melted butter and Parmesan.

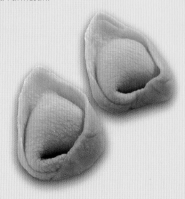

Venus' navel supposedly served as the model for shapely tortellini.

The triangle is curved around the forefinger and the tip of the triangle folded in. Finally, the ends of the dough are joined in a ring.

The pasta dough is rolled out thin and cut first into strips, then into squares.

Filling is placed in the centre of each square, which is then folded into a triangle.

Tortellini ai funghi
Mushroom Tortellini

For the dough:

1 g saffron strands
300 g/11 oz Italian flour, plus extra for dusting
1 egg and 1 egg white
2 tbsp oil
½ tsp salt
1 tbsp vinegar

For the filling:

2 tbsp butter
2 shallots, finely chopped
1 garlic clove, finely chopped
300 g/11 oz button mushrooms or wild mushrooms, finely chopped
2 tbsp finely chopped parsley
1 tsp dried thyme
2 tbsp grated Parmesan
salt and pepper

Soak the saffron in 2 tablespoons of hot water. Place the flour in a bowl, press a hollow in the centre and pour the saffron water into it through a sieve. Add the egg, egg white, oil, salt and vinegar and knead into a silky, smooth dough. Add a little water as needed. Wrap the dough in clingfilm and chill in the refrigerator for 1 hour.

For the filling, melt the butter in a frying pan, add the shallots, garlic and mushrooms, and sauté on medium heat until all the liquid evaporates. Blend in the parsley and season with the thyme, salt and pepper. Leave the mushroom mixture to cool slightly, then stir in the Parmesan. Put the mixture in the refrigerator to chill.

Thinly roll out the pasta dough. Cut it into 6-cm/2½-inch squares with a pastry wheel and place a little of the filling in the middle of each square. Fold each square into a triangle, being sure to securely close the edges of the dough over the filling.

Wind each triangle around your fore-finger. Curve the tip and lay the other two corners over your finger. Clasp the ends into a ring and press them firmly together. Set the tortellini on a floured tea towel to dry for 30 minutes. Bring a large saucepan of lightly salted water to the boil. Add the tortellini and cook until al dente.

Ravioli al formaggio
Ravioli with Feta Cheese

For the dough:

300 g/11 oz Italian flour, plus extra for dusting
2 eggs
1 tbsp oil
½ tsp salt
1 tsp vinegar
3–4 tbsp water

For the filling:

250 g/9 oz feta cheese
2 garlic cloves, finely chopped
2 tbsp finely chopped parsley
1 fresh red chilli, cored and finely chopped
salt and pepper

Knead the flour, eggs, oil, salt, vinegar and water into a silky, smooth dough. Wrap the dough in clingfilm and chill in the refrigerator for 1 hour.

For the filling, crumble the cheese and combine it with the garlic, parsley and chilli. Season to taste with salt and pepper. Prepare the ravioli in the same way as for the following recipe, *Ravioli alla zucca*.

Ravioli alla zucca
Pumpkin-filled Ravioli

For the dough:

300 g/11 oz Italian flour, plus extra for dusting
2 eggs
1 tbsp oil
½ tsp salt
1 tsp vinegar
3–4 tbsp water

For the filling:

1 tbsp olive oil
500 g/1 lb 2 oz pumpkin, cubed
1 shallot, finely diced
50 g/1¾ oz grated Parmesan
1 egg
1 tbsp finely chopped parsley
salt and pepper

Knead the flour, eggs, oil, salt, vinegar and water into a silky, smooth dough. Wrap the dough in clingfilm and chill in the refrigerator for 1 hour.

For the filling, heat the olive oil in a frying pan and sauté the pumpkin and shallot until the shallot is translucent. Add 125 ml/4 fl oz water and cook the pumpkin until the liquid evaporates. Cool slightly, then mix with the Parmesan, egg, parsley, and salt and pepper.

Divide the dough in half. Thinly roll out both pieces. Place small spoonfuls of the pumpkin mixture about 4 cm/1½ inches apart on one sheet of pasta. Brush a little water on the spaces in between. Lay the second sheet on top and press down around each piece of filling. Use a pastry wheel to cut out squares, then press their edges together with a fork. Set aside the ravioli to dry for 30 minutes, then bring a large saucepan of lightly salted water to the boil. Add the ravioli and cook over medium heat until al dente. Remove them with a slotted spoon and drain well on paper towels.

Panzerotti al gambero
Panzerotti Stuffed with Prawns

250 g/9 oz flour, plus extra for dusting
2 eggs
5 tbsp olive oil
1 tbsp wine vinegar
300 g/11 oz raw prawns
40 ml/2½ tbsp brandy
250 ml/9 fl oz white wine
300 g/11 oz tomatoes
1 onion, diced
1 garlic clove, finely chopped
1 tbsp balsamic vinegar
5 spring onions, chopped
1 celery stick, diced
2 tbsp finely chopped parsley
sugar
salt and pepper
celery leaves to garnish

Knead together the flour, eggs, 1 tablespoon of olive oil, vinegar, 1–2 tablespoons of water and a pinch of salt into a silky, smooth dough. Wrap the dough in clingfilm and chill in the refrigerator for 2 hours.

Wash the prawns and drain them. Heat 1 tablespoon of oil in a frying pan and fry the prawns briefly on all sides until they turn pink. Then remove from the pan and leave them to cool.

Shell and de-vein the prawns. Finely chop the heads and shells and brown in the pan for 2 minutes. Pour in the brandy and wine, then vigorously boil down the resulting stock. Pour off the liquid through a fine sieve and set it aside.

Peel and quarter the tomatoes, remove the seeds, and dice. Heat the remaining oil in a clean frying pan and sauté the onion and garlic. Add the tomatoes and cook briefly. Pour in the stock, stir, then season to taste with the vinegar, sugar, salt and pepper. Simmer on low heat until the sauce thickens.

Dice the prawns. Combine with the spring onions and celery, and add salt and pepper.

Thinly roll out the dough on a floured work surface. Cut out 10-cm/4-inch circles of dough. Use a teaspoon to place grape-sized portions of the filling on the dough circles. Fold half of the dough over the filling so that it forms a semicircle. With a fork, press the edges together around the filling.

Place portions of the panzerotti in boiling salted water and cook on medium heat for 3 to 4 minutes. Remove with a slotted spoon and transfer into the sauce. Sprinkle with the chopped parsley and garnish with celery leaves to serve.

Sauté the prawns briefly in olive oil until they turn pink. Then remove from the shells.

Stew the tomatoes with onion and garlic, then pour in the prawn stock.

Cut circles out of the sheet of dough. Put a little filling in the centre of each. Fold the dough over into semicircles.

Cook the panzerotti in boiling, salted water for several minutes, then remove with a slotted spoon.

Lasagne

As with so many Italian dishes, the most famous baked pasta, *lasagne*, has ancient Roman roots. The writer Horace raved about *lagani*, thin sheets of pasta made from water and flour. He enjoyed eating the pasta with chickpeas and leeks. *Lasagne e ceci*, lasagne with chickpeas, is still a very popular dish in Basilicata today.

Proficient home cooks and good restaurants prepare their lasagne with home-made pasta. The pasta dough is thinly rolled out, then cut into strips 10 cm (4 inches) wide and the same length as the baking dish in which the lasagne will be made. After letting the pasta dry for a while, it can be used uncooked. Store-bought lasagne is faster and easier, and it is also available ready to use without precooking.

Lasagne is a culinary delight. It consists of alternating layers of pasta, vegetables, meat or fish, and sauce. Tomato sauce provides a fresh, juicy taste, while a bechamel sauce makes the lasagne creamy and also gives it firmness. Mozzarella or Parmesan make for a crisp, cheesy crust when it is grilled.

Garlic

This aromatic, healthy bulb was long considered to be poor people's food. In fact, noblemen who smelled of garlic were denied entry at court. But in the end, the little white or red garlic bulb finally did find its way into fine cuisine, at least in Italy. Not only the pungent aroma, but also the health benefits of garlic are indisputable. Its intense odour, perceived by some to be unpleasant, comes from the essential oil that is released not only via the breath, but also through the pores of the skin after it is eaten.

Lasagne con verdure e coda di rospo
Vegetable Lasagne with Monkfish

100 g/3½ oz butter, plus extra for greasing
2 onions, diced
1 tbsp flour
150 ml/5 fl oz fish stock
125 ml/4 fl oz dry vermouth
500 ml/18 fl oz double cream
2 egg yolks
1 tbsp spicy mustard
juice of 1 lemon
2–3 leeks, sliced
3 courgettes, diced
4 carrots, diced
1 fennel bulb, diced
80 g/3 oz breadcrumbs
2 garlic cloves, finely chopped
2 tbsp finely chopped parsley
12 lasagne noodles
500 g/1 lb 2 oz monkfish fillets
1 handful fresh dill, finely chopped
salt and pepper

Heat half the butter and sauté the onion, then dust with the flour. Pour in the fish stock and vermouth and simmer for 10 minutes. Stir in the cream and cook 10 minutes more. Remove from the heat and bind with the egg yolk. Season with salt, pepper, mustard and lemon juice. Preheat the oven to 200°C/390°F/gas mark 6 and grease a baking dish with butter.

Blanch the vegetables and drain. In a bowl, mix them with half of the sauce. Fry the garlic and breadcrumbs in the remaining butter until golden brown. Mix in the parsley.

Cover the base of the baking dish with a thin layer of sauce. Layer lasagne noodles, half the vegetables and half the breadcrumbs. Top with another layer of pasta. Arrange the fish on the pasta, season with salt, pepper and dill, and pour a little sauce over it. Then cover with more lasagne noodles, the remainder of the vegetables and a little of the breadcrumb mixture, and finish with a layer of noodles. Pour the rest of the sauce over top, sprinkle on the left-over breadcrumbs and bake for 20 to 25 minutes.

Lasagne verde al forno
Green Lasagne with Minced Beef

2 tbsp olive oil, plus extra for greasing
1 onion, diced
2 garlic cloves, finely chopped
1 carrot, diced
1 celery stick, diced
400 g/14 oz minced beef
500 g/1 lb 2 oz canned tomato purée
2 tsp dried oregano
600 ml/1 pint béchamel sauce
12 green lasagne noodles, ready to use without precooking
300 g/11 oz mozzarella, thinly sliced
50 g/1¾ oz grated Parmesan
salt
freshly ground pepper

Preheat the oven to 200°C/390°F/gas mark 6 and grease a rectangular baking dish. Heat the olive oil in a frying pan and sauté the onion, garlic, carrots and celery, then add the mince and brown it, stirring often. When the meat has browned, mix in the tomatoes, season with salt, pepper and oregano, and simmer for 15 minutes.

Heat the béchamel sauce and cover the base of the baking dish with a thin layer of it. Alternate a layer of lasagne noodles with a layer of meat sauce, then mozzarella slices, followed by lasagne noodles and béchamel sauce until all the ingredients have been used. Finally, cover the top of the lasagne with béchamel sauce and sprinkle with the Parmesan. Bake for 25 to 30 minutes. Wait 5 minutes before cutting the lasagne.

Trenette al forno con tonno
Baked Trenette with Tuna Fish

370 g/13 oz canned tuna and vegetables
500 g/1 lb 2 oz canned tomato purée
1 tsp dried oregano
1 tbsp finely chopped parsley
350 g/12 oz trenette pasta
300 g/11 oz mozzarella, diced
2 tomatoes, sliced
salt
freshly ground pepper

Preheat the oven to 200°C/390°F/gas mark 6 and grease a baking dish. Drain the tuna and vegetables in a sieve, then use a fork to flake the fish. Heat the tomato purée in a saucepan, add the tuna and simmer for a few minutes. Remove the sauce from the heat and season with oregano, parsley, salt and pepper.

Bring a large saucepan of lightly salted water to the boil. Add the pasta and cook according to packet instructions until al dente. Drain well. Spread one-third of the sauce in the base of the baking dish. Layer half of the pasta and half the mozzarella on top, then pour in another third of the sauce and add the remaining pasta. Spread the remaining sauce over the pasta and cover with sliced tomatoes. Layer the remaining mozzarella on top and bake the casserole for approximately 30 minutes.

Cannelloni agli spinaci
Spinach Cannelloni

600 g/1 lb 5 oz spinach
1½ tbsp butter
1 small onion, finely chopped
200 g/7 oz ricotta cheese
12 cannelloni,
ready to use without precooking
600 ml/1 pint bechamel sauce
50 g/1¾ oz grated Parmesan
salt
freshly ground pepper
freshly grated nutmeg

Preheat the oven to 200°C/390°F/gas mark 6 and grease a baking dish. Wash the spinach thoroughly and remove any wilted leaves and coarse stalks. Heat the butter in a saucepan and sauté the onion until it is translucent. Add the spinach while still dripping wet, cover the pan and leave it to wilt. Drain the spinach well in a sieve, then chop it.

Combine the spinach and ricotta, then add salt, pepper and nutmeg to taste. Transfer the spinach mixture into a piping bag with a large nozzle and use it to fill the cannelloni.

Lay the filled cannelloni side by side in the baking dish, cover with the bechamel sauce and sprinkle with the Parmesan. Bake for 25 to 30 minutes.

Pasta e lenticchie
Pasta with Lentils

150 g/5 oz Castellucio lentils
50 g/1¾ oz pancetta, diced
4 tbsp olive oil
1 small onion, finely chopped
2 garlic cloves, finely chopped
1 celery stick, diced
1 carrot, diced
500 ml/18 fl oz vegetable stock
1 bay leaf
1 sprig rosemary
200 g/7 oz short macaroni
salt
freshly ground pepper
2 tbsp finely chopped parsley

Rinse the lentils and drain them. Heat the olive oil and render the bacon. Lightly sauté the onion and garlic in the oil and bacon fat. Add the celery and carrot to the pan, cook a few minutes, then add the lentils, stock, bay leaf and rosemary. Simmer on low heat for about 40 minutes. Discard the bay leaf and rosemary. Bring a large saucepan of lightly salted water to the boil. Add the macaroni and cook it until al dente. Drain the pasta and combine it with the lentils. Season with salt and pepper and sprinkle with the parsley.

Schlutzkrapfen
Filled Pasta Pockets

150 g/5 oz rye flour
100 g/3½ oz wholemeal flour
1 egg
1 tbsp olive oil
300 g/11 oz spinach
150 g/5 oz butter
1 small onion, finely chopped
1 garlic clove, finely chopped
100 g/3½ oz quark (curd cheese)
100 g/3½ oz Parmesan, grated
freshly grated nutmeg
salt and pepper
snipped chives to garnish

Knead together both flours, the egg, olive oil and 3–4 tablespoons of lukewarm water into a smooth dough. Form it into a ball, wrap in clingfilm and set aside for 30 minutes. Wash the spinach. While still dripping wet, heat it in a covered saucepan briefly until it wilts. Drain well, then chop finely. Heat 1 tablespoon of butter and sauté the onion and garlic. Remove from the heat and mix in the spinach, quark and 1 tablespoon of Parmesan. Season with nutmeg, salt and pepper.

Roll out the dough as thin as possible in a pasta machine. Cut out circles 7 cm/2¾ inch in diameter. Place a little spinach filling on each circle, moisten the edges with water and fold the dough over the filling to form a semicircle. Press the edges together. Cook until al dente in gently boiling salted water.

Brown the remaining butter and pour it over the *Schlutzkrapfen*. Sprinkle with the remaining Parmesan and the chives.

Vincisgrassi
Marche-style Lasagne

100 g/3½ oz butter
100 g/3½ oz pancetta, diced
1 small onion, diced
1 carrot, diced
300 g/11 oz chicken giblets
50 ml/1½ fl oz white wine
1 tbsp tomato purée
100 ml/3½ fl oz meat stock
⅛ tsp cinnamon
20 g/¾ oz dried ceps
125 ml/4 fl oz milk
400 ml/14 fl oz béchamel sauce
12 lasagne noodles, ready to use without precooking
75 g/2½ oz grated Parmesan
salt
freshly ground pepper

Heat the butter in a deep frying pan and render the pancetta. Add the onion and carrot and sauté. Chop the giblets, setting aside the liver. Add the other giblets to the pan, fry briefly, then deglaze with the wine. Stir the tomato purée into the stock and add to the meat in the pan. Season with the cinnamon, and salt and pepper to taste. Cover and simmer on low heat for about 1 hour. Soak the ceps in lukewarm water.

Pour the water off the ceps, squeeze out excess liquid and cut the mushrooms into small pieces. Add them to the pan along with the chopped chicken liver and milk. Mix everything well, then simmer for 30 minutes.

Grease a rectangular baking dish and pre-heat the oven to 200°C/390°F/gas mark 6. Heat the béchamel sauce and cover the base of the dish with a thin layer of it. Alternate lasagne noodles with chicken sauce, followed by noodles and béchamel sauce until all ingredients have been used. Spread béchamel sauce on top of the lasagne and sprinkle with Parmesan. Bake for 25 to 30 minutes. Wait 5 minutes before cutting the lasagne.

Gnocchi, Polenta & Risotto

Gnocchi

Gnocchi are a classic part of Italian cuisine and, particularly in northern and central Italy, a popular first course. Despite the simplicity of the ingredients from which they are made, they are a delicacy. Connoisseurs declare that they taste best *au naturel* with nothing more than a little melted butter and freshly grated Parmesan; yet it would be a shame to forego all the other delicious gnocchi dishes.

Gnocchi probably originated in Lombardy in association with the pre-Lenten carnival celebrations. Traditionally, gnocchi were prepared by the man of the house and eaten with butter, tomato sauce or with sugar and cinnamon.

Cooking perfect gnocchi is an art form that requires some time. They must be fluffy, yet retain their shape during cooking. Almost no one achieves this on their first try.

Preparation of the dough demands an instinctive feel, because there are no precise guidelines for the ingredients. The amount of flour needed for the dough depends on the amount of starch in the potatoes, and will range between 200 and 350 grams of flour per kilogram (3–5 oz per pound) of potatoes. To make the best possible gnocchi, use fully ripe baking potatoes and allow the steam to escape from them before putting them through a potato press.

The shape of the gnocchi is just as important as the choice of the right potatoes. Genuine gnocchi must have grooves or indentations so they are better able to pick up the butter or sauce. This is accomplished either by rolling each gnocchi over the back of a fork or by pressing them against the inside of a cheese grater. Gnocchi that are made in factories generally have a smooth surface, which is a peccadillo in the eyes of traditionalists.

Basic Gnocchi Recipe

1 kg/2 lb 4 oz baking potatoes
1 egg
2 egg yolks
300 g/11 oz flour
salt

Bring a saucepan of salted water to the boil and cook the potatoes for about 25 minutes. Then pour off the water. Cool the potatoes slightly, peel them and put through a potato press while still hot. Leave them to cool further and salt lightly.

Knead together the potatoes, egg and egg yolks. Work in as much flour as needed to produce a smooth, supple dough that does not stick to your fingers. The amount of flour will vary depending on the type of potatoes used. On a floured work surface, form finger-width rolls or logs from the potato dough. Cut the logs into pieces 2–3 cm/³⁄₄–1 inch long and gently roll each one over the back of a fork to give the gnocchi their characteristic texture. Bring a large saucepan of salted water to the boil and cook the gnocchi, in portions, until they rise to the surface. Remove with a slotted spoon, drain and prepare according to the desired recipe.

Gnocchi di zucca mantovani
Mantua-style Pumpkin Gnocchi

500 g/1 lb 2 oz pumpkin flesh
150 g/5 oz flour
50 g/1¾ oz amaretti crumbs
2 eggs
1 pinch salt
75 g/2½ oz butter, melted
75 g/2½ oz grated Parmesan

Preheat the oven to 200°C/390°F/gas mark 6. Dice the pumpkin, place it in a baking dish and bake for 45 minutes. Press the pumpkin through a sieve while it is still hot. Add the flour, amaretti crumbs, eggs and a pinch of salt to the pumpkin and knead thoroughly into a smooth, supple dough. On a floured work surface, form finger-width rolls. Cut them into pieces about 2–3 cm/³⁄₄–1 inch long and gently roll each one over the back of a fork. Bring a large saucepan of salted water to the boil and cook the gnocchi, in portions, until they rise to the surface. Remove with a slotted spoon, drain and drizzle each serving with melted butter and sprinkle with grated Parmesan.

To make gnocchi dough, boil the potatoes, remove the skins and put through a potato press while still hot.

Knead the potato with egg, egg yolks and as much flour as needed to produce a smooth, supple dough.

Divide the dough into portions on a floured surface and form into finger-width rolls.

Cut off small pieces from the roll of potato dough with a sharp knife or a cleaver.

Roll the gnocchi over the back of a fork to give them texture, and cook in boiling salted water.

The gnocchi are done when they rise to the surface. Remove from the water with a slotted spoon.

Drain the gnocchi and when all are cooked toss them in a tomato sauce.

Simmer briefly in the sauce, then sprinkle with freshly grated Parmesan.

Mushrooms, The Finest of Companions

Italians love the flavourful wild mushrooms that grow in the cool, moist forests of northern and central Italy. They accompany almost every course on the menu. Fresh ceps are served as finely sliced carpaccio for appetizers, as are mixed mushrooms marinated with herbs in oil and vinegar. In Tuscany, aromatic mushroom butter is a favourite to spread on white toast. Risotto, pasta and polenta taste especially fine with a flavourful mushroom sauce. For a second course, mushrooms can demonstrably stand alone or as equals with meat and poultry.

Gathering mushrooms is an ancient practice in the history of mankind. Mushrooms were an important component of seasonal nutrition, and not only in Italy. They are rich in high-quality vegetable protein, contain important minerals and are low in calories, although the latter hardly played a role in times gone by.

Unlike in many northern European countries, mushroom hunting is strictly regulated in Italy by regional laws. Anyone who wants to gather mushrooms needs to have an official permit, which is issued by municipalities for a fee.

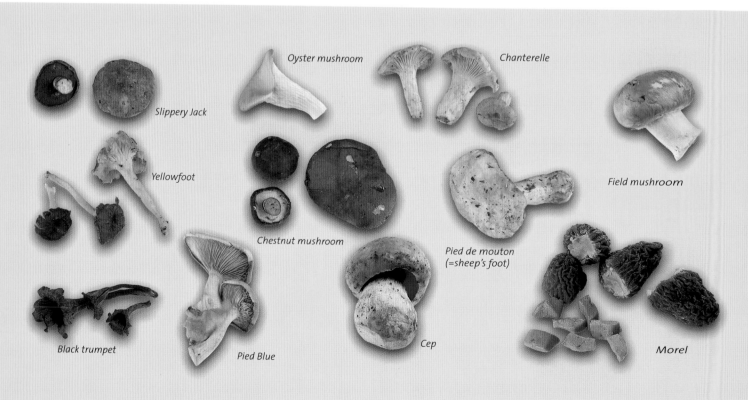

Slippery Jack

Oyster mushroom

Chanterelle

Yellowfoot

Field mushroom

Chestnut mushroom

Pied de mouton
(=sheep's foot)

Black trumpet

Pied Blue

Cep

Morel

Risotto ai funghi porcini
Risotto with Ceps

300 g/11 oz ceps
75 g/2½ oz prosciutto
3 tbsp butter
2 shallots, finely chopped
300 g/11 oz risotto rice
250 ml/9 fl oz Prosecco
1 litre/1¾ pints meat stock
1 tbsp finely chopped parsley
75 g/2½ oz grated Parmesan
salt
freshly ground pepper

Clean and finely slice the ceps. Finely dice the prosciutto.

Melt half of the butter in a saucepan. Fry the shallots and diced prosciutto in the butter. Sprinkle the rice in the pan and continue to cook. Deglaze the pan with the Prosecco. Heat the meat stock in a separate saucepan. When the wine has nearly evaporated, pour in one third of the hot stock, stirring continuously until the liquid is absorbed. Repeat this process twice more.

Meanwhile, melt the rest of the butter and sauté the mushrooms, then add them to the risotto. Season to taste with salt and pepper. Sprinkle each serving with parsley and serve the Parmesan on the side.

Picture credits

The publisher would like to thank the following for permission to reproduce copyright material.

All product photographs and cutouts: Martin Kurtenbach, Jürgen Schulzki, Ruprecht Stempell. All other photographs Martin Kurtenbach.

Except the following:

Gunter Beer: all wood backgrounds; 8 (top left); 13 (top right); 14; 15; 16; 17; 24; 25 (top); 26; 27; 32 (top & bottom right); 39 (top); 42; 43; 45; 52; 55; 59; 60; 66; 68; 69; 72 (all except top right); 77 (right); 79 (top); 80 (top); 82; 85; 88-9; 90; 91; 92 (top right); 93; 95

2 Gunter Beer; 6 Hussenot/photocuisine; 8 Mike Cooper (except top left); 10-11 Cultura (large); 25 (box) Jürgen Schulzki; 58 (top) Ruprecht Stempell; 58 (bottom) Enzo & Paolo Ragazzini; 32 (bottom left) Don Last; 34-35 Hulton-Deutsch; 129 (top) Atlantide Phototravel; 40-41 Atlantide Phototravel; 57 Atlantide Phototravel; 60 (box) Ruprecht Stempell; 61 Hussenot/photocuisine; 62 (all) Don Last; 63 Mascarucci; 64 (top left) Ruprecht Stempell; 67 (box) Ruprecht Stempell; 76 (large) Grand Tour; 80 (bottom) ditter.projektagentur GmbH; 83 Guido Baviera/Grand Tour; 84 (large) Bob Krist; 86-7 (large) Ruprecht Stempell; 94 Botanik Bildarchiv Laux

Front cover: ditter.projektagentur GmbH (Venice); Gunter Beer (pizza); Sebastiano Scattolin/Grand Tour (Tuscany); Gunter Beer (gnocchi); Riccardo Spila/Grand Tour (Baia dei Turchi); Atlantide Phototravel (Sicily); Gunter Beer (risotto); Gunter Beer (pizza); Grand Tour (Trieste)

Back cover: Gunter Beer